FUNDAMENTALS OF APPLIED PHYSICS–I

UNITS AND MEASUREMENTS, FORCE AND MOTION, WORK, POWER AND ENERGY, ROTATIONAL MOTION, PROPERTIES OF MATTER, HEAT AND THERMOMETRY

MR. GOPAL CHAKRABORTY
DR. SAIKAT MAJUMDER
MR. NIRATYAY BISWAS

Dedicated

to

The memory of my beloved father

Late Sankar Chakraborty

(Father of Mr. Gopal Chakraborty)

&

To the memory of my beloved father

Late Samarendra Majumder

(Father of Dr. Saikat Majumder)

&

and to my beloved mother

Ms. Sourabhi Biswas

(Mother of Mr. Niratyay Biswas)

Their honesty and devotion to education is ever rememberable

Contents

Foreword

This book namely "Fundamentals of Applied Physics-I" *contain the chapter like* **Physical world, Units and Measurements, Force and Motion, Work, Power and Energy, Rotational Motion, Properties of Matter, Heat and Thermometry** *. It has been written with a view to cater the need of undergraduate Engineering students. This book is written strictly in accordance with the new syllabus introduced by West Bengal State Council of Technical and Vocational Education and Skill Development for the 1st Semester Students of Diploma Engineering (Polytechnic).*

Preface

This book on "Fundamentals of Applied Physics-I" has been written with a view to cater the need of undergraduate Engineering students. This newly edition of book is written strictly in accordance with the new syllabus introduced by West Bengal State Council of Technical and Vocational Education and Skill Development for the 1st Semester Students of Diploma Engineering (Polytechnic).

This book is thoroughly revised and addition and alteration of Chapters and exercises have been done for the benefits of students, I hope this edition will also be well accepted by my respected teachers and my beloved students.

The book has been written in very lucid and simple English. While presenting the subject matter, it has been my constant conscious effort to give more depth of treatment and emphasis on the fundamentals. In doing so, I have deliberately avoided the unnecessary experimental complications on the one hand and undue mathematical treatment on the other. To illustrate the applications of the basic principles of the concept developed, in more or less simple form, numerous problems and multiple choice type questions have been appended towards the end of each Module.

I hope, this publication will also be response equally well by respected teachers and my beloved students like previous editions of this book. Any suggestions, comments and constructive criticism of this first edition of this book are cordially invited and thank fully acknowledged both from students and teachers for further improvement of this book.

Prologue

WBSCTVESD Curriculum for Diploma Courses in Engineering and Technology

Syllabus of Applied Physics for Semester-I (Theory)

Reviewed and prepared by Syllabus-Sub-committee, on the basis of recommendation of AICTE

Semester –I (Theory)
Course Code: BS103
Course Title: Applied Physics-I
Number of credits: 3 (L: 2, T: 1, P: 0)
Prerequisites: High School Level Physics
Course Category: BS (Basic Science)

Course Content:

Unit 1: Physical world, Units and Measurements

Physical quantities; fundamental and derived, Units and systems of units (CGS and SI units),

Dimensions and dimensional formulae of physical quantities, Principle of homogeneity of dimensions, Dimensional equations and their applications (conversion from one system of units to other, checking of dimensional equations and derivation of simple equations), Limitations of dimensional analysis.

Measurements: Need, measuring instruments, least count, types of Measurement (direct, indirect), Errors in Measurements (systematic and random), absolute error, relative error, error propagation, error estimation and significant figures.

Unit 2: Force and Motion

Force, Momentum, Conservation of linear momentum, its applications such as recoil of gun, numerical problems rockets (concept only), Impulse and impulsive force.

Circular motion, definition of angular displacement, angular velocity, angular acceleration, frequency, time period, relation between linear and angular velocity, linear acceleration and angular acceleration (related numerical), concept of Centripetal and centrifugal forces with examples (No derivation, only formula) banking of roads and bending of cyclist, concept and formula and numerical problems.

Unit 3: Work, Power and Energy

Work: Concept and units, examples of zero work, positive and negative work

Friction: concept, types, laws of limiting friction, coefficient of friction, reducing friction and its engineering applications, Work done in moving an object on rough inclined plane.

Energy and its units, kinetic energy and potential energy, Conservation of mechanical energy for freely falling bodies (simple numerical problems), transformation of energy (examples only).

Power and its units, power and work relationship, calculation of power (numerical problems).

Unit 4: Rotational Motion

Translational and rotational motion with examples, Definition of torque and angular momentum and their relation, Conservation of angular momentum (quantitative) and its applications.

Moment of inertia and its physical significance, radius of gyration for rigid body, Theorems of parallel and perpendicular axes (statements only), Moment of inertia of rod, disc, ring and sphere (hollow and solid); (Formulae only). Simple numerical problems.

Unit 5: Properties of Matter

Elasticity: definition of stress and strain, moduli of elasticity, Hooke's law, significance of stress-strain curve.

Surface tension: Concept, units, cohesive and adhesive forces, angle of contact, Capillary rise (formula only), applications of surface tension, effect of temperature and impurity on surface tension.

Viscosity and coefficient of viscosity: terminal velocity, Stoke's law and effect of temperature on viscosity.

Hydrodynamics: Fluid motion, stream line and turbulent flow, Reynold's number Equation of continuity, Bernoulli's Theorem (only formula and numerical problem) and its applications (mention name only).

Unit 6: Heat and Thermometry

Concept of heat and temperature, basic concepts of measurements of heat and temperature, modes of heats transfer (conduction, convection and radiation with examples), Co-efficient of thermal conductivity simple numerical problems.

Expansion of solids, liquids and gases, coefficient of linear, surface and cubical expansions of solids and relation amongst them, specific heats Cp & Cv of a gas and their relationship (Mention only).

PROLOGUE

Syllabus of Applied Physics for Semester-I (Lab)

Reviewed and prepared by Syllabus-Sub-committee, on the basis of recommendation of AICTE

Applied Physics for Semester-I (Lab)
Course Code: BS107
Course Tittle: Applied Physics-I Labs
Numbers of Credits: 1 (L: 0, T: 0, P: 2)
Prerequisites: NIL
Course Category: BS (Basic Science)
Course Objectives:

Study of Applied Physics aims to give an understanding of physical world by observations and predictions. Concrete use of physical principles and analysis in various fields of engineering and technology is very prominence. The course aims to supplement the factual knowledge gained in the lecture by first hand manipulation of apparatus. This will develop scientific temper and help to apply the basic concepts and principles in solving engineering and technology based problems. In addition, students get necessary confidence in handling equipment and thus learn various skills in measurement.

List of Practical's/Activities (To perform minimum 8 practicals).

1. To measure the volume of the material of a given hollow cylinder, using a Slide Callipers.
2. To determine the area of cross section of a thin wire using a screw gauge.
3. To determine radius of curvature of a convex and a concave mirror/ surface using a Spherometer.
4. To find the co-efficient of friction between wood and glass using a horizontal board.
5. To determine force constant of a spring using Hook's law.
6. To find the moment of inertia of a flywheel.
7. To find the viscosity of a given liquid (Glycerine) by Stoke's law
8. To find the co-efficient of linear expansion of the material of a rod.
9. To verify Boyle's law.
10. To determine the relative density of sand by using a sp. gr. Bottle.

PROLOGUE

Semester Examination Question Format

(As per examination held on May, 2025)

QUESION CODE

SUBJECT NAME

Time Allowed: 2.5 Hours Full Marks: 60

Answer to Question No. 1 of Group A must be written in the main answer script.

In Question No. 1, out of 2 marks for each MCQ, 1 marks is allotted for right answer and 1 marks is allotted for correct explanation of the answer.

Answer any Five (05) Questions from Group-B.

GROUP-A

1. Choose the correct answer from the given alternatives and explain your answer (any ten): 2x10=20

Guidelines:

i. Total number of questions will be set=15

ii. Total number of questions to be answered=10

GROUP-B

Answer any Five (05) questions.

Question No 2 to 9/10: 8x5

Guidelines:

i. Total number of questions will be set=8/9

ii. Total number of questions to be answered=5

iii. Total Marks of each question=8 (with any combination of marks e.g. 3+5, 4+4, 2+6 etc.)

Note: Question format of Semester Examination may change anytime as per notification of WBSCTVE&SD.

PROLOGUE

Overview of Chapters

CONTENTS

Unit 1: Physical world, Units and Measurements

Unit 2: Force and Motion

Unit 3: Work, Power and Energy

Unit 4: Rotational Motion

Chapter-1: Physical world, Units and Measurements

Unit 1: Physical world, Units and Measurements

Physical quantities; fundamental and derived, Units and systems of units (CGS and SI units),

Dimensions and dimensional formulae of physical quantities, Principle of homogeneity of dimensions, Dimensional equations and their applications (conversion from one system of units to other, checking of dimensional equations and derivation of simple equations), Limitations of dimensional analysis.

Measurements: Need, measuring instruments, least count, types of Measurement (direct, indirect), Errors in Measurements (systematic and random), absolute error, relative error, error propagation, error estimation and significant figures.

Physical World

1.1 What is Science?

It is a systematised and organised knowledge about the various natural phenomena which is obtained by careful experimentation, keen observation and accurate reasoning. The Sanskrit word "Shastra" and Arabic word "Ilm" also have a similar meaning i.e., organised knowledge.

1.2 What are physical and biological sciences?

Two types of sciences. The knowledge of science can be divided into two broad categories:

i. **Biological sciences.** The sciences which deal with the behaviour of living things are called biological sciences. These sciences include Botany, Zoology, Ornithology, Anthropology, Entomology, Forensic Science, etc.

ii. **Physical sciences.** The two main physical sciences are physics and chemistry. Chemistry is the study of every substance, its structure, its composition and changes in which it takes part. Physics is the study of the natural world which deals with the concepts of space, time, motion, matter, energy, radiation, etc. Other physical sciences include Geology, Geography, Astronomy, Astrology, Oceanology, etc.

1.3 What is Physics?

Physics, the word physics originates from a Greek word which means nature, this word was introduced by ancient scientist Aristotle in the year 350 B.C. The Sanskrit equivalent of physics is bhautiki which refers to the physical world. Physics is the branch of science that deals with the study of basic laws of nature and their manifestation in various natural phenomena. It is concerned with the interaction of matter with matter or energy. It deals with the various features of the natural world such as space, time, matter, motion, energy, radiation, etc. Physics is the most fundamental of all sciences as it is concerned with the study of various natural phenomena.

1.4 What are the two basic quests in physics?

Two principal thrusts in physics are unification and reductionism.

1. **Unification:** In physics, attempt is made to explain various physical phenomena in terms of just - few concepts and laws. We try to see the physical world as manifestation of some universal laws. For example, the same (Newton's) law of gravitation can be used to describe the motion of a body falling towards the earth, motion of the moon around the earth and motion of planets around the sun. Attempts are being made to unify fundamental forces of nature in the pursuit of unification.

2. **Reductionism:** Another attempt made in physics is to explain a macroscopic system in terms of its microscopic constituents. This pursuit is called reductionism. For example, thermodynamics was

developed to explain the macroscopic properties such temperature, internal energy, entropy, etc., of the bulk systems. Later on, these properties were explained in terms of molecules in kinetic theory and statistical mechanics.

1.5 What are the scopes of Physics?

The scope of physics is very wide. Every event, which occurs around us in our daily life, is governed by one or the other principle of physics. One way of getting the idea of the scope of physics is to look at its various sub-disciplines. Another way is look at the vast range of magnitude of the physical quantities it deals with.

1.6 Main disciplines and sub-disciplines in physics:

Physics has two main domains of study-macroscopic and microscopic.

Classical physics deals with macroscopic phenomena which may be at the laboratory, terrestrial and astronomical scales. It includes branches like mechanics, optics, thermodynamics and electrodynamics.

Quantum mechanics deals with microscopic phenomena at the minute scales of atoms, molecules and nuclei.

Main sub-disciplines in physics

1. **Mechanics:** It deals with the equilibrium or motion of material bodies at low speeds. It is based on laws of gravitation. The propulsion of rocket, equilibrium of rod bent under a load, propagation of water waves or sound waves in air, etc., are studied in mechanics.
2. **Optics:** It deals with the nature and propagation of light. It deals with the formation of images by mirrors and lenses, colours in thin films, etc.
3. **Thermodynamics:** It deals with a macroscopic System in equilibrium and is concerned with the changes in internal energy, temperature, entropy, etc., of the system through external work and heat. Here we study the efficiency of heat engines and refrigerators.
4. **Electrodynamics:** It deals with electric and magnetic phenomena associated with charged and magnetic bodies. It is based on laws given by Coulomb, Oersted, Ampere and Faraday, which were later on unified by Maxwell. It deals with problems like motion of current-carrying

conductor in a magnetic field, propagation of radio waves through the atmosphere, etc.

5. **Quantum mechanics:** It deals with the mechanical behaviour of sub-microscopic particles like atoms and nuclei and their interaction with projectiles like electrons, photons and other elementary particles.

6. **Relativity:** It is theory of invariance in nature. It deals with the motion of the particles having speeds comparable to the speed of light.

Measurements and Units

1.7 Needs for the Measurement

Physics is an exact science which gives an accurate knowledge about the nature and the natural phenomena. It expresses various natural phenomena in terms of the relation- ships among the quantities involved. The exactness or accuracy of these relationships depends upon the measurements we make. The accuracy of the measurements, in turn, depends on the accuracy of the measuring instruments and techniques. The recent progress in science and technology has been possible only due to the development of high precision instruments. One can measure mass as small as that of an electron (~10-30 kg) and as large as that of the universe (-10 kg). Prof. William S. Franklin emphasised the importance of measurement in the following words: "The most important thing for a young man to acquire from his first course in physics is an appreciation for precise details."

1.8 The Measuring Process

The measurement of a physical quantity is the process of comparing this quantity with a standard amount of the physical quantity of the same kind, called its unit.

To express the measurement of a physical quantity we need to know two things:

1. The unit in which the quantity is measured.
2. The numerical value or the magnitude of the quantity i.e., the number of times that unit is contained in the given physical quantity.

Measure of a physical quantity = Numerical value of the physical quantity x size of the unit

$$\text{Or } Q = NU$$

Let length of a room = 5 m=500 cm. Clearly, the smaller the size of the unit, the larger is the numerical value associated with the physical quantity.

Thus the numerical value (n) is inversely proportional to the size (u) of the unit.

$N \propto 1/U$

or $NU = Constant$

If N_1 and N_2, are numerical values for a physical quantity Q corresponding to the units U_1 and U_2, then

$$Q = N_1 U_1 = N_2 U_2$$

1.9 Physical Quantities

All those quantities which can be measured directly or indirectly and in terms of which the laws of physics can be expressed are called physical quantities.

For example, length, mass, temperature, speed, force, electric current, etc. The physical quantities are the building blocks of physics in terms of which the basic laws of physics can be expressed in mathematical forms.

Physical quantities are of two types – fundamental and derived.

Fundamental quantities: The physical quantities which can be treated as independent of other physical quantities and are not usually defined in terms of other physical quantities are called fundamental quantities. To give a consistent and unambiguous description to all physical quantities, we need a minimum of seven fundamental or base quantities, these are mass, length, time, electric current, temperature, luminous intensity and amount of substance.

Derived quantities: The physical quantities whose defining operations is based on other physical quantities are called derived quantities. All physical quantities other than the seven base quantities are derived quantities. For example, velocity, acceleration, force, momentum, etc.

1.10 Physics Unit

The standard amount of a physical quantity chosen to measure the physical quantity of the same kind is called a physical unit.

Desirable characteristics of a physical unit:

1. It should be well-defined.
2. It should be of convenient size, i.e., neither too small nor too large in comparison with the measurable physical quantity.
3. It should not change with time.
4. It should be easily reproducible.
5. It should be imperishable or indestructible
6. It should not be affected by the change in physical conditions such as pressure, temperature, etc.
7. It should be internationally acceptable.
8. It should be easily accessible.

1.11 Fundamental Unit & Derived Unit

Fundamental units: The physical units which can neither be derived from one another, nor they can be further resolved into simpler units are called fundamental units. The units of fundamental quantities such as mass, length, etc. are fundamental units.

e.g. Fundamental Physical Quantity Fundamental unit

Mass Kg, Gram, Pound

Length Metre, Centimetre, Foot

Time Second

Derived units: All the other physical units which can be expressed in terms of the fundamental units are called derived units.

Let us consider the unit of speed,

Speed = Distance travelled/ Time taken

Unit of speed = Unit of distance/ Unit of time =metre/ second= ms^{-1}

Thus the unit of speed (ms^{-1}) is a derived unit as it has been expressed in the fundamental units of length and time.

Or Unit of Area = Length x Breadth

= Length x Length

= $(Length)^2$= $Metre^2$

1.12 System of Units

A complete set of units which is used to measure all kinds of fundamental and derived quantities is called a system of units.

Some of the commonly used systems of units are as follows:

i. **CGS system:** It was set up in France. It is based on centimetre, gram and second as the fundamental units of length, mass and time respectively.

ii. **FPS system:** It is a British system based on foot, pound and second as the fundamental units of length, mass and time respectively.

iii. **MKS system:** It is also a French system based on metre, kilogram and second as the fundamental units of length, mass and time respectively.

iv. **SI:** The international system of units. SI is the abbreviation for "*Systeme Internationale d' Unites*", which is French equivalent for international system of units. It is a modernised and extended form of the metric systems like cgs and mks systems. This system was adopted by eleventh General Conference of Weights and Measures in 1960. It covers all branches of science and technology. t is based on the following seven basic units and two supplementary units.

1.13 Definition of all the basic and supplementary units of SI.

The seven basic SI units are defined as follows:

Metre (m): It is the SI unit of length. One metre is defined as the length of the path travelled by light in vacuum during a time interval of 1/299, 792, 458 of a second

i. **Kilogram (kg):** It is the SI unit of mass. One kilogram is the mass of prototype cylinder of platinum-iridium alloy (whose height is equal to its diameter) preserved at the International Bureau of Weights and Measures, at Sevres, near Paris.

ii. **Second (s):** It is the SI unit of time. One second is the duration of 9, 192, 631, 770 periods of the radiation corresponding to the transition between two hyperfine levels of the ground state of the caesium -133 atom.

iii. **Ampere (A):** It is the SI unit of electric current. One ampere is that constant current which, if maintained in two straight parallel conductors of infinite length, of negligible cross-section, and placed 1 metre apart in vacuum, would produce between these conductors a force equal to 2 x 10^{-7} newton per metre of length.

iv. **Kelvin (K):** It is the SI unit of temperature. One kelvin is the fraction 1/273.16 of the thermodynamic temperature of the triple point of water. The triple point of water is the temperature at which ice, water and water vapour co-exist.

v. **Candela (cd):** It is the SI unit of luminous intensity. One candela is the luminous intensity, in a given direction, of a source that emits monochromatic radiation of frequency 540x 10^{12} hertz and that has a radiant intensity of 1 / 683 watt per steradian in that direction.

vi. **Mole (mol):** One mole is that amount of a substance which contains as many elementary entities as there are atoms in 0.012 kg of carbon-12 isotope. The entities may be atoms, molecules, ions etc.

The two supplementary SI units are defined as follows:

a. **Radian (rad):** It is defined as the plane angle subtended at the centre of a circle by an arc equal in length to the radius of the circle.

θ in radians=Arc/ Radius=1/r

a. **Steradian (sr):** It is defined as the solid angle subtended at the centre of a sphere by a surface of the sphere equal in area to that of a square, having each side equal to the radius of the sphere.

Ω in radians=Surface Area/ Radius2

1.14 Coherent system of Units

It is a system of units based on a certain set of fundamental units from which all derived units can be obtained by simple multiplication or division without introducing any numerical factor.

For example mks system is a coherent system of units in mechanics. All derived units in mechanics such as those of area, volume, density, acceleration, force, etc., can be obtained by the multiplication or division of the fundamental units of mass, length and time. SI is a coherent system of units for all branches of physics.

1.15 Advantages of SI over other systems of units

i. **SI is a coherent system of units.** All derived units can be obtained by simple multiplication or division of fundamental units without introducing any numerical factor.

ii. **SI is a rational system of units.** It uses only one unit for a given physical quantity. For example, all forms of energy are measured in joule. On the other hand, in mks system, the mechanical energy is measured in joule, heat energy in calorie and electrical energy in watt hour.

iii. **SI is a metric system.** The multiples and submultiples of SI units can be expressed as powers of 10.

iv. **SI is an absolute system of units.** It does not use gravitational units. The use of 'g is not required.

v. **SI is an internationally accepted system of units.**

1.16 Guidelines for writing SI Units in symbols

i. Rules for writing SI units in symbolic form:
ii. Small letters are used for symbols of units.
iii. Symbols are not followed by a full stop.
iv. The initial letter of a symbol is capital only when the unit is named after a scientist.
v. The full name of a unit always begins with a small letter even if it has been named after a scientist.
vi. Symbols do not take plural form

Table of Fundamental Units

Sr. No.	Name of Physical Quantity	Unit	Symbol
1	Length	Metre	m
2	Mass	Kilogram	Kg
3	Time	Second	s
4	Temperature	Kelvin	K
5	Electric Current	Ampere	A
6	Luminous Intensity	Candela	Cd
7	Quantity of Matter	Mole	mol

Table of Supplementary unit

Sr. No	Name of Physical Quantity	Unit	Symbol
1	Plane angle	Radian	rad
2	Solid angle	Steradian	sr

Fig. 1.1

SOME IMPORTANT ABBREVIATIONS

Symbol	Prefix	Multiplier	Symbol	Prefix	Multiplier
D	Deci	10^{-1}	da	deca	10^{1}
c	centi	10^{-2}	h	hecto	10^{2}
m	milli	10^{-3}	k	kilo	10^{3}
μ	micro	10^{-6}	M	mega	10^{6}
n	nano	10^{-9}	G	giga	10^{9}
P	Pico	10^{-12}	T	tera	10^{12}
f	femto	10^{-15}	P	Pecta	10^{15}
a	atto	10^{-18}	E	exa	10^{18}

Fig 1.2

Some Important Units of Length:

1 micron = 10^{-6} m = 10^{-4} cm

1 angstrom = 1Å = 10^{-10} m = 10^{-8} cm

1 fermi = 1 fm = 10^{-15} m

1 Light year = 1 ly = 9.46 x 10^{15} m

1 Parsec = 1pc = 3.26 light year

Some conversion factor of mass:

1 Kilogram = 2.2046 pound

1 Pound = 453.6 gram

1 kilogram = 1000 gram

1 milligram = 1/1000 gram = 10^{-3} gram

1 centigram = 1/100 gram = 10^{-2} gram

1 decigram = 1/10 gram

1 quintal = 100 kg

1 metric ton = 1000 kilogram

1.17 Dimensions

The powers, to which the fundamental units of mass, length and time written as M, L and T are raised, which include their nature and not their magnitude.

For example Area = Length x Breadth

$= [L^1] \times [L^1] = [L^2] = [M^0L^2T^0]$

Power (0, 2, 0) of fundamental units are called dimensions of area in mass, length and time respectively.

e.g. Density = mass/volume = $[M^1]/[L^3]$ = $[M^1L^{-3}T^0]$

Velocity = $[M^0L^1T^{-1}]$

Dimensional formula SI& CGS unit of Physical Quantities

Sr. No.	Physical Quantity	Formula	Dimensions	Name of S.I unit
1	Force	Mass × acceleration	$[M^1L^1T^{-2}]$	Newton (N)
2	Work	Force × distance	$[M^1L^2T^{-2}]$	Joule (J)
3	Power	Work / time	$[M^1L^2T^{-3}]$	Watt (W)
4	Energy (all form)	Stored work	$[M^1L^2T^{-2}]$	Joule (J)
5	Pressure, Stress	Force/area	$[M^1L^{-1}T^{-2}]$	Nm^{-2}
6	Momentum	Mass × velocity	$[M^1L^1T^{-1}]$	$Kgms^{-1}$
7	Moment of force	Force × distance	$[M^1L^2T^{-2}]$	Nm
8	Impulse	Force × time	$[M^1L^1T^{-1}]$	Ns
9	Strain	Change in dimension / Original dimension	$[M^0L^0T^0]$	No unit
10	Modulus of elasticity	Stress / Strain	$[M^1L^{-1}T^{-2}]$	Nm^{-2}
11	Surface energy	Energy / Area	$[M^1L^0T^{-2}]$	$Joule/m^2$
12	Surface Tension	Force / Length	$[M^1L^0T^{-2}]$	N/m
13	Co-efficient of viscosity	Force × Distance/ Area × Velocity	$[M^1L^{-1}T^{-1}]$	N/m^2
14	Moment of inertia	Mass × (radius of gyration)^2	$[M^1L^2T^0]$	$Kg\text{-}m^2$
15	Angular Velocity	Angle / time	$[M^0L^0T^{-1}]$	Rad.per sec
16	Frequency	1/Time period	$[M^0L^0T^{-1}]$	Hertz
17	Area	Length × Breadth	$[M^0L^2T^0]$	$Metre^2$
18	Volume	Length × breadth × height	$[M^0L^3T^0]$	$Metre^3$
19	Density	Mass/ volume	$[M^1L^{-3}T^0]$	Kg/m^3
20	Speed or velocity	Distance/ time	$[M^0L^1T^{-1}]$	m/s
21	Acceleration	Velocity/time	$[M^0L^1T^{-2}]$	m/s^2
22	Pressure	Force/area	$[M^1L^{-1}T^{-2}]$	N/m^2

Fig 1.3

1.18 Classification of Physical Quantity:

Physical quantity has been classified into following four categories on the basis of dimensional analysis.

i. **Dimensional Constant:** These are the physical quantities which possess dimensions and have constant (fixed) value. e.g. Planck's constant, gas constant, universal gravitational constant etc.

ii. **Dimensional Variable:** These are the physical quantities which possess dimensions and do not have fixed value. e.g. velocity, acceleration, force etc.

iii. **Dimensionless Constant:** These are the physical quantities which do not possess dimensions but have constant (fixed) value. e.g. e,? , ?????????? 1,2,3,4,5 etc.

iv. **Dimensionless Variable:** These are the physical quantities which do not possess dimensions and have variable value. e.g. angle, strain, specific gravity etc.

Example 1. Derive the dimensional formula of following Quantity & write down their dimensions.

i.   (i) Density (ii) Power (iii) Co-efficient of viscosity (iv) Angle
Sol. (i) Density = mass/volume
$= [M]/[L^3] = [M^1L^{-3}T^0]$
(ii) Power = Work/Time
= Force x Distance/Time
$= [M^1L^1T^{-2}] \times [L]/[T]$
$= [M^1L^2T^{-3}]$
(iii) Co-efficient of viscosity
Coefficient of viscosity=(Force x Distance)/ (Area x Velocity)=(Mass x Acceleration x Distance x time)/ (Length x length x Displacement)= $[M] \times [LT^{-2}] \times [L] [T]/[L^2] \times [L] = [M^1L^{-1}T^{-1}]$

ii. (iv) Angle= arc (length)/radius (length)
iii. $= [L]/[L]$
$= [M^0L^0T^0]$ = no dimension

Example 2. Explain which of the following pair of physical quantities have the same dimension:

i.   (i) Work & Power (ii) Stress & Pressure (iii) Momentum &Impulse
Sol. (i) Dimension of work = force x distance = $[M^1L^2T^{-2}]$
Dimension of power = work / time = $[M^1L^2T^{-3}]$
Work and Power have not the same dimensions.
(ii) Dimension of stress = force / area = $[M^1L^1T^{-2}]/[L^2] = [M^1L^{-1}T^{-2}]$
Dimension of pressure = force / area = $[M^1L^1T^{-2}]/[L^2] = [M^1L^{-1}T^{-2}]$

Stress and pressure have the same dimension.

(iii) Dimension of momentum = mass x velocity= $[M^1L^1T^{-1}]$

Dimension of impulse = force x time = $[M^1L^1T^{-1}]$

1.19 Principle of Homogeneity of Dimensions

It states that the dimensions of all the terms on both sides of an equation must be the same. According to the principle of homogeneity, the comparison, addition & subtraction of all physical quantities is possible only if they are of the same nature i.e., they have the same dimensions.

If the power of M, L and T on two sides of the given equation are same, then the physical equation is correct otherwise not. Therefore, this principle is very helpful to check the correctness of a physical equation.

Example: A physical relation must be dimensionally homogeneous, i.e., all the terms on both sides of the equation must have the same dimensions.

In the equation, $S = ut + 1/2\ at^2$

The length (S) has been equated to velocity (u) & time (t), which at first seems to be meaningless, But if this equation is dimensionally homogeneous, i.e., the dimensions of all the terms on both sides are the same, then it has physical meaning.

Now, dimensions of various quantities in the equation are:

Distance, $S = [L^1]$

Velocity, $u = [L^1T^{-1}]$

Time, $t = [T^1]$

Acceleration, $a = [L^1T^{-2}]$

½ is a constant and has no dimensions.

Thus, the dimensions of the term on L.H.S. is $S = [L^1]$ and

Dimensions of terms on R.H.S.

$ut + 1/2\ at^2 = [L^1T^{-1}]\ [T^1] + [L^1T^{-2}]\ [T^2] = [L^1] + [L^1]$

Here, the dimensions of all the terms on both sides of the equation are the same. Therefore, the equation is dimensionally homogeneous.

1.20 Dimensional Equations, Applications of Dimensional Equations

Dimensional Analysis: A careful examination of the dimensions of various quantities involved in a physical relation is called dimensional analysis. The analysis of the dimensions of a physical quantity is of great help to us in a number of ways as discussed under the uses of dimensional equations.

Uses of dimensional equation: The principle of homogeneity & dimensional analysis has put to the following uses:

(i) Checking the correctness of physical equation.

(ii) To convert a physical quantity from one system of units into another.

(iii) To derive relation among various physical quantities.

1. To check the correctness of Physical relations: According to principle of Homogeneity of dimensions a physical relation or equation is correct, if the dimensions of all the terms on both sides of the equation are the same. If the dimensions of even one term differs from those of others, the equation is not correct.

Example 3. Check the correctness of the following formulae by dimensional analysis.

(i) ?=?v^2/r

Where all the letters have their usual meanings.

Sol. ?=??$^?$/?

Dimensions of the term on L.H.S

Force, F = $[M^1L^1T^{-2}]$

Dimensions of the term on R.H.S

??$^?$/? = $[M^1][L^1T^{-1}]^2 / [L]$

= $[M^1L^2T^{-2}]/[L]$

= $[M^1L^1T^{-2}]$

The dimensions of the term on the L.H.S are equal to the dimensions of the term on R.H.S. Therefore, the relation is correct.

(ii) ?=??√?/?

Here, Dimensions of L.H.S, t = $[T^1]$ = $[M^0L^0T^1]$

Dimensions of the terms on R.H.S

Dimensions of (length) = $[L^1]$

Dimensions of g (acceleration due to gravity) = $[L^1T^{-2}]$

2? being constant have no dimensions.

Hence, the dimensions of terms 2?√?/? on R.H.S

= $([L^1/ L^1T^{-2}])^{1/2}$ = $[T^1]$ = $[M^0L^0T^1]$

Thus, the dimensions of the terms on both sides of the relation are the same i.e., $[M^0L^0T^1]$.Therefore, the relation is correct.

Example 4. Check the correctness of the following equation on the basis of dimensional analysis, ?=√?/?. Here V is the velocity of sound, E is the elasticity and d is the density of the medium.

Sol. Here, Dimensions of the term on L.H.S

$V = [M^0L^1T^{-1}]$

Dimensions of elasticity, $E = [M^1L^{-1}T^{-2}]$

& Dimensions of density, $d = [M^1L^{-3}T^0]$

Therefore, Dimensions of the terms on R.H.S

$\sqrt{?}/? = [M^1L^{-1}T^{-2}/ M^1L^{-1}T^{-2}]^{1/2} = [M^0L^1T^{-1}]$

Thus, dimensions on both sides are the same, therefore the equation is correct.

Example 5. Using Principle of Homogeneity of dimensions, check the correctness of equation,

h = 2Td /rgCos?.

Sol. The given formula is, h = 2Td /rgCos?.

Dimensions of term on L.H.S

Height (h) = $[M^0L^1T^0]$

Dimensions of terms on R.H.S

T= surface tension = $[M^1L^0T^{-2}]$

D= density = $[M^1L^{-3}T^0]$

r =radius = $[M^0L^1T^0]$

g=acc. due to gravity = $[M^0L^1T^{-2}]$

Cos? = $[M^0L^0T^0]$= no dimensions

So,

Dimensions of 2Td/rgCos? = $[M^1L^0T^{-2}]$ x $[M^1L^{-3}T^0]$ / $[M^0L^1T^0]$ x $[M^0L^1T^{-2}]$

= $[M^2L^{-5}T^0]$

Dimensions of terms on L.H.S are not equal to dimensions on R.H.S. Hence, formula is not correct.

Example 6. Check the accuracy of the following relations:

(i) E = mgh + ½ mv²; (ii) v³-u² = 2as².

Sol. (i) E = mgh + ½ mv²

Here dimensions of the term on L.H.S.

Energy, E = $[M^1L^2T^{-2}]$

Dimensions of the terms on R.H.S,

Dimensions of the term, mgh = $[M] \times [LT^{-2}] \times [L] = [M^1L^2T^{-2}]$

Dimensions of the term, ½ mv2= $[M] \times [LT^{-1}]^2= [M^1L^2T^{-2}]$

Thus, dimensions of all the terms on both sides of the relation are the same, therefore, the relation is correct.

(ii) The given relation is, v³-u²= 2as²

Dimensions of the terms on L.H.S

$v^3 = [M^0] \times [LT^{-1}]^3= [M^0L^3T^{-3}]$

$u^2 = [M^0] \times [LT^{-1}]^2 = [M^0L^2T^{-2}]$

Dimensions of the terms on R.H.S

$2as^2 = [M^0] \times [LT^{-2}] \times [L]^2 = [M^0L^3T^{-2}]$

Substituting the dimensions in the relations, $v^3-u^2 = 2as^2$

We get, $[M^0L^3T^{-3}] - [M^0L^2T^{-2}] = [M^0L^3T^{-2}]$

The dimensions of all the terms on both sides are not same; therefore, the relation is not correct.

Example 7. The velocity of a particle is given in terms of time t by the equation v = At + b/t+c

What are the dimensions of a, b and c?

Sol. Dimensional formula for L.H.S

$V = [L^1T^{-1}]$

In the R.H.S dimensional formula of At

$[T] = [L^1T^{-1}]$

$A = [LT^{-1}] / [T^{-1}] = [L^1T^{-2}]$

t +c = time, c has dimensions of time and hence is added in t.

Dimensions of t + c is $[T]$

Now, b / t + c = v

$b = v (t + c) = [LT^{-1}] [T] = [L]$

There dimensions of a= $[L^1T^{-2}]$, Dimensions of b = $[L]$ and that of c = $[T]$

Example 8. In the gas equation (P + a/v2) (v – b) = RT, where T is the absolute temperature, P is pressure and v is volume of gas. What are dimensions of a and b?

Sol. Like quantities are added or subtracted from each other i.e.

$(P + a/v^2)$ has dimensions of pressure = $[ML^{-1}T^{-2}]$

Hence, a/v^2 will be dimensions of pressure = $[ML^{-1}T^{-2}]$

$a = [ML^{-1}T^{-2}] [volume]^2 = [ML^{-1}T^{-2}] [L^3]^2$

$a = [ML^{-1}T^{-2}] [L^6] = [ML^5T^{-2}]$

Dimensions of a = $[ML^5T^{-2}]$

$(v – b)$ have dimensions of volume i.e.,

b will have dimensions of volume i.e., $[L^3]$

or $[M^0L^3T^0]$

2. To convert a physical quantity from one system of units into another.

Physical quantity can be expressed as

$Q = nu$

Let n_1u_1 represent the numerical value and unit of a physical quantity in one system and n_2u_2 in the other system.

If for a physical quantity Q; $M_1L_1T_1$ be the fundamental unit in one system and $M_2L_2T_2$ be fundamental unit of the other system and dimensions in mass, length and time in each system can be respectively a,b,c.

$$u_1 = [\, M_1{}^a L_1{}^b T_1{}^c\,]$$

and

$$u_2 = [\, M_2{}^a L_2{}^b T_2{}^c\,]$$

as we know

$$n_1 u_1 = n_2 u_2$$

$$n_2 = n_1 u_1 / u_2$$

$$n_2 = n_1 \frac{\left[M_1^a L_1^b T_1^c \right]}{\left[M_2^a L_2^b T_2^c \right]}$$

$$n_2 = n_1 \left[\left(\frac{M_1}{M_2} \right)^a \left(\frac{L_1}{L_2} \right)^b \left(\frac{T_1}{T_2} \right)^c \right]$$

Enter Caption

While applying the above relations the system of unit as first system in which numerical value of physical quantity is given and the other as second system.

Thus knowing $[M_1L_1T_1]$, $[M_2L_2T_2]$ a, b, c and n_1, we can calculate n_2

Example 9. Convert a force of 1 Newton to dyne.

Sol. To convert the force from MKS system to CGS system, we need the equation

$Q = n_1 u_1 = n_2 u_2$

Thus $n_2 = \dfrac{n_1 u_1}{u_2}$

Here $n_1 = 1$, $u_1 = 1N$, $u_2 = $ dyne

$$n_2 = n_1 \frac{\left[M_1 L_1 T_1^{-2} \right]}{\left[M_2 L_2 T_2^{-2} \right]}$$

$$n_2 = n_1 \left(\frac{M_1}{M_2} \right)\left(\frac{L_1}{L_2} \right)\left(\frac{T_1}{T_2} \right)^{-2}$$

$$n_2 = n_1 \left(\frac{kg}{gm} \right)\left(\frac{m}{cm} \right)\left(\frac{s}{s} \right)^{-2}$$

$$n_2 = n_1 \left(\frac{1000\,gm}{gm} \right)\left(\frac{100\,cm}{cm} \right)\left(\frac{s}{s} \right)^{-2}$$

$$n_2 = 1(1000)(100)$$

$$n_2 = 10^5$$

Thus **$1N = 10^5$ dynes**.

Fig 1.4

Example 10.Convert work of 1 erg into Joule.

Sol: Here we need to convert work from CGS system to MKS system. Thus in the equation

$$n_2 = \frac{n_1 u_1}{u_2}$$

$n_1 = 1$

u_1=erg (CGS unit of work)

u_2= joule (SI unit of work)

$$n_2 = \frac{n_1 u_1}{u_2}$$

$$n_2 = n_1 \frac{M_1 L_1^2 T_1^{-2}}{M_2 L_2^2 T_2^{-2}}$$

$$n_2 = n_1 \left(\frac{M_1}{M_2}\right)\left(\frac{L_1}{L_2}\right)^2\left(\frac{T_1}{T_2}\right)^{-2}$$

$$n_2 = n_1 \left(\frac{gm}{kg}\right)\left(\frac{cm}{m}\right)^2\left(\frac{s}{s}\right)^{-2}$$

$$n_2 = n_1 \left(\frac{gm}{1000gm}\right)\left(\frac{cm}{100cm}\right)^2\left(\frac{s}{s}\right)^{-2}$$

$$n_2 = 1(10^{-3})(10^{-2})^2 \quad n_2 = 10^{-7}$$

Thus, **1 erg= 10^{-7} Joule**.

Fig 1.5

1.21 Limitations of Dimensional Equation:

The method of dimensions has the following limitations:

1. It does not help us to find the value of dimensionless constants involved in various physical relations. The values, of such constants have to be determined by some experiments or mathematical investigations.
2. This method fails to derive formula of a physical quantity which depends upon more than three factors. Because only three equations are obtained by comparing the powers of M, L and T.
3. It fails to derive relations of quantities involving exponential and trigonometric functions.
4. The method cannot be directly applied to derive relations which contain more than one terms on one side or both sides of the equation, such as v= u + at or s = ut + ½ at^2 etc. However, such relations can be derived indirectly.

A dimensionally correct relation may not be true physical relation because the dimensional equality is not sufficient for the correctness of a given physical relation.

1.22 Errors in Measurement

Errors in Measurements are a common phenomenon in any method. The result of every measurement done with the help of any measuring instrument contains some uncertainty. This uncertainty is called error. In any physical or mathematical system, there is always a calibrated scale to measure a physical quantity. When it is measured a numerical value is read from this predefined scale.

Definition of Error

An error is a fault, which may occur even in the most careful observation. Or Error is a deviation of measurement from standard value. Or error is an uncertainty in a given measurement. Error arises due to human limitations and instrumental limitations. Errors cannot be completely eliminated but can be reduced.

Types of Errors

In Physics errors are basically the deviation of the actual value from the calculated ones, and they are classified as given below:

1. **Systematic Error:** these are the errors due to the system. Systematic error is further classified as

2. Instrumental error: Errors that arise due to imperfect design or calibration of the measuring instrument. Eg: Zero error in Vernier callipers emerges when the zero marks of the Vernier scale may not coincide with the zero marks of the main scale, An ordinary meter scale may be worn off at one end.

3. Error in measuring technique: To determine the temperature of a human body, a thermometer placed under the armpit will always give a temperature lower than the actual value of the body temperature.

4. Environmental Errors: Environmental Errors are due to connections external to the measuring device, including conditions in the area surrounding the instrument, such as the effects of change in temperature, humidity, barometric pressure, or of magnetic or electrostatic fields.

5. Personal errors: that arise due to an individual's bias, lack of proper setting of the apparatus or an individual's carelessness in taking down observations

6. **Random errors:** Random errors are those errors, which occur irregularly and hence are random with respect to sign and size. These can arise due to random and unpredictable fluctuations in experimental conditions. For example: if a person takes multiple readings for the same experiment it is possible that every reading taken would be unique and different from others.

7. **Least count error:** The smallest value that can be measured by the measuring instrument is called its least count. For example, a Vernier calliper has the least count of 0.01cm; a spherometer may have the least count of 0.001 cm. Using instruments of higher precision, improving experimental techniques, etc., we can reduce the least count error.

1.22.1 Errors

True value: Since the true value cannot be absolutely determined, in practice an accepted reference value is used. The accepted reference value is usually established by repeatedly measuring some NIST or ISO traceable reference standard. This value is not the reference value that is found published in a reference book. Such reference values are not "right" answers; they are measurements that have errors associated with them as well and may not be totally representative of the specific sample being measured.

Accuracy is the closeness of agreement between a measured value and the true value.

Error is the difference between a measurement and the true value of the measure and (the quantity being measured).

Precision is the closeness of agreement between independent measurements of a quantity under the same conditions. It is a measure of how well a measurement can be made without reference to a theoretical or true value.

Absolute Error

Absolute error is defined as the difference between the True Value or actual value and the measured value of a quantity. The importance of absolute error depends on the quantity that we are measuring. If the quantity is large such as road distance, a small error in centimetres is negligible. While measuring the length of a machine part an error in centimetre is considerable. Though the errors in both cases are in centimetres, the error in the second case is more important.

The absolute error is calculated by the subtraction of the True value and the measured value of a quantity. If the actual value is X^0 and the measured value is X, the absolute error is expressed as,

$\Delta X = X^0 - X$

Here, Δx is the absolute error.

Example

Here, we are giving an example of the absolute error in real life. Suppose, we are measuring the length of an eraser. The actual length is 45 mm and the measured length is 44.10 mm.

So, the Absolute Error = Actual Length - Measured Length = (45 - 44.10) mm = 0.90 mm

Mean Absolute Error

Mean Absolute Error or the mean absolute error is the mean or average of all absolute errors. The formula for Mean Absolute Error is given as,

$$Mean\ Absolute\ Error = \frac{1}{n}\sum_{i=1}^{n} |X_i - X|$$

Relative Error or Proportional Error

The ratio of absolute error of the measurement and the actual value is called relative error. By calculating the relative error, we can have an idea of how good the measurement is compared to the actual size. From the relative error, we can determine the magnitude of absolute error. If the actual value is not available, the relative error can be calculated in terms of the measured value of the quantity. The relative error is dimensionless and it has no unit. It is written in percentage by multiplying it by 100.

The relative error is calculated by the ratio of absolute error and the True value of the quantity. If the absolute error of the measurement is ΔX, the actual value is X_0, the measured value is X, the relative error is expressed as, Relative Error or Proportional Error= Absolute Error/ True Value

$$Xr = (X^0 - X)/ X^0 = \Delta X/X^0$$

Here, Xr is the relative error.

Example: Here, we are giving an example of relative error in real life. Suppose, the actual length of an eraser is 35 mm. Now, the absolute error = (45 - 44.10) mm = 0.90 mm

So, the relative error = absolute error/actual length = 0.90/45 = 0.02

Percentage Error= Relative Error or Proportional Error x 100%

1.23 Significant figures

The significant figures of a given number are those significant or important digits, which convey the meaning according to its accuracy. For example, 6.658 has four significant digits. These substantial figures provide precision to the numbers. They are also termed as significant digits.

The number of significant figures in a result is simply the number of figures that are known with some degree of reliability. The number 13.2 is said to have 3 significant figures. The number 13.20 is said to have 4 significant figures. Significant figures are critical when reporting scientific data because they give the reader an idea of how well you could actually measure/report your data.

Rules for Significant Figures

1. All non-zero digits are significant. 198745 contains six significant digits.
2. All zeros that occur between any two nonzero digits are significant. For example, 108.0097 contains seven significant digits.

3. All zeros that are on the right of a decimal point and also to the left of a non-zero digit is never significant. For example, 0.00798 contained three significant digits.

4. All zeros that are on the right of a decimal point are significant, only if, a non-zero digit does not follow them. For example, 20.00 contains four significant digits.

5. All the zeros that are on the right of the last non-zero digit, after the decimal point, are significant. For example, 0.0079800 contains five significant digits.

6. All the zeros that are on the right of the last non-zero digit are significant if they come from a measurement. For example, 1090 m contains four significant digits.

Rounding Significant Figures

A number is rounded off to the required number of significant digits by leaving one or more digits from the right. When the first digit in left is less than 5, the last digit held should remain constant. When the first digit is greater than 5, the last digit is rounded up. When the digit left is exactly 5, the number held is rounded up or down to receive an even number. When more than one digit is left, rounding off should be done as a whole instead of one digit at a time.

There are two rules to round off the significant numbers:

1. First, we have to check, up to which digit the rounding off should be performed. If the number after the rounding off digit is less than 5, then we have to exclude all the numbers present on the right side.

2. But if the digit next to the rounding off digit is greater than 5, then we have to add 1 to the rounding off digit and exclude the other numbers on the right side.

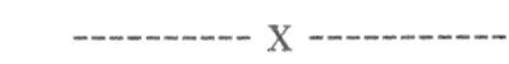

1.24 Important Short Questions & Answers:

1. **What is a unit?**

A unit is a standard quantity used for measuring a physical quantity. For example, the meter (m) is the unit of length.

2. What are fundamental units?

Fundamental units are the base units upon which all other units are defined. Examples include meter (length), kilogram (mass), second (time), and ampere (electric current).

3. **What are the fundamental units of length, mass, and time in the SI system?**

Length: Meter (m)
Mass: Kilogram (kg)
Time: Second (s)

4. **What are derived units?**

Derived units are formed by combining fundamental units. Examples include speed (meter/second), force (kilogram x meter/second^2), and density (kilogram/meter^3).

5. **Explain the principle of dimensional homogeneity.**

The principle states that an equation is dimensionally homogeneous if all the terms in the equation have the same dimensions. For example, if an equation relates length, time, and velocity, the dimensions of the terms must be consistent (e.g., length / time = velocity).

6. **What are some practical applications of units and measurements in daily life?**

Measuring the length of cloth, the volume of water, or the weight of groceries.

Understanding scientific concepts like speed, acceleration, and force.

7. **What is the importance of choosing appropriate units for measurements?**

Choosing the right units helps to avoid errors and ensures that measurements are consistent and comparable.

8. **Give some examples of Unit less physical quantities:**

Ratios: Strain (change in length divided by original length), Refractive Index, Specific Gravity.
Percentages: Mass percent, volume percent.
Mole fraction: The ratio of the number of moles of a component to the total number of moles in a mixture.

9. **Give some examples of Dimension less physical quantities**

Strain, Specific Gravity, Refractive Index, Relative Humidity, Plane Angle (radian), Solid Angle (Steradian).

10. **Give an example of a physical quantity which has unit but no dimension.**

An example of a physical quantity that has a unit but no dimension is angle, specifically measured in radians or degrees. While the unit radian is used to quantify an angle, it's actually derived from the ratio of arc length to radius, which are both lengths and thus cancel out when forming the ratio, resulting in a dimensionless quantity.

11. **Give an example of a physical quantities which has same unit.**

Work and Energy, Impulse and Linear Momentum, Torque and Work.
1.25 Important Numerical Questions & Answers:

1. **If the time period (t) of a simple pendulum depends on its length (l), mass of bob (m), angular displacement (?) and acceleration due to gravity (g). Find out the expression of time period of pendulum by dimensional analysis.**

Let us consider

$t \propto l^a \Theta^b m^c g^d$

or $t = k l^a \Theta^b m^c g^d$, where k is a dimensionless constant. Taking dimension of both side,

$[M^0 L^0 T^0] = [L^a][M^c][LT^{-2}]^d = [L^{a+d} M^c T^{-2d}]$
Now comparing the power of M, L & T from both side we get,
a+d=0, a=-d
c=0,
And -2d=1, d=-1/2, hence a=1/2
Substituting the value of a,c,d we get $?=k\sqrt{?}/?$
As we know k=2π, therefore $?=2\pi \sqrt{?}/?$

2. **The centripetal force F acting on a particle moving uniformly in a circle may depend upon mass (m), velocity (v) and radius (r) of the circle. Derive the formula for F using the method of dimensions.**

$$F \propto m^a v^b r^c$$

$$F = k m^a v^b r^c$$

Where k is a dimensionless constant. Taking dimension of both side,
$[M^1 L^1 T^{-2}] = [M^a][LT^{-1}]^b[L^c] = [M^a L^{b+c} T^{-b}]$
Now comparing the power of M, L & T from both side we get,
a=1, b+c=1 and b=2, therefore c=-1
Substituting the value of a,c,d we get $F=kmv^2 r^{-1}=kmv^2/r$

3. **If the units of force, length and time are taken as fundamental units. What would be the dimension of mass?**

Let the dimension of mass (M), depends on force (F), length (L) and Time (T)
$M = F^a L^b T^c$
Putting dimension of both side we get,

$[M^1L^0T^0] = [MLT^{-2}][L]^b[T]^c = [M^aL^{a+b}T^{-2a+c}]$

Since the dimension of both sides are equal, comparing the power of M, L & T from both side we get,

a=1, a+b=0 and -2a+c=0

Therefore a=1, b=-1, c=2

Substituting the value of a,c,d we get $M=FL^{-1}T^2$

4. **A current (2.00±0.01)A is passing through a resistance (100±0.02)Ω. Find the potential difference across the resistance with error limits.**

We know V=IR=2x100=200 volt.

Hence Proportional error in potential,

dV/V= dI/I+dR/R

=0.01/2+0.2/100

=0.005+0.002=0.007

Hence dV=0.007 x V=0.007 x 200=1.4 volt.

Potential difference with error limit is (200± 1.4) volt.

5. **A current (2.00±0.01)A is passing through a resistance (100±0.02)Ω. Find out the percentage error in power using formula P=I²R.**

$P=I^2R$

Hence Proportional error is dP/P= 2dI/I+dR/R = 2x 0.01/2+0.2/100

=0.012

Now Percentage error= Proportional error x 100%

= 0.012x100%

= 1.2%

6. **To find are (A) of a circle of radius r=5 cm, the readings obtained for measurement of radius are 4.9 cm, 4.95 cm, 5.1 cm and 5.05 cm. Find maximum percentage error and the proportional error in the measurement of area.**

Area of circle A= πr^2

Now we know, dA/A=2dr/r

Absolute error in radius, dr=|4.9-5|=|5.1-5|=0.1

And dr=|4.95-5|=|5.05-5|=0.05

Maximum absolute error is dr=0.1

Maximum proportional error in Area is dA/A=2dr/r=2x0.1/5=0.04

Maximum percentage error in Area=0.04x100%=4%

7. **A new system of units is proposed in which unit of mass is α kg, unit of length β m and unit of time λ s. How much will 5 J measure in this new system?**

Let the physical quantity be $Q = n_1 u_1 = n_2 u_2$

Let M_1, L_1, T_1 and M_2, L_2, T_2 be units of mass, length and time in the given two systems.

So, $n_2 = n_1 \left[\dfrac{M_1}{M_2}\right]^a \times \left[\dfrac{L_1}{L_2}\right]^b \times \left[\dfrac{T_1}{T_2}\right]^c$

We know that dimension of energy $[U] = [ML^2T^{-2}]$

According to the problem, $M_1 = 1$ kg, $L_1 = 1$ m, $T_1 = 1$ s

$M_2 = \alpha$ kg, $L_2 = \beta$ m, $T_2 = \gamma$ s

Substituting the values, we get

$$n_2 = 5\left[\dfrac{M_1}{M_2}\right] \times \left[\dfrac{L_1}{L_2}\right]^2 \times \left[\dfrac{T_1}{T_2}\right]^{-2}$$

$$= 5\left[\dfrac{1}{\alpha}\,kg\right] \times \left[\dfrac{1}{\beta}\,m\right]^2 \times \left[\dfrac{1}{\gamma}\,s\right]^{-2}$$

$$= 5 \times \dfrac{1}{\alpha} \times \dfrac{1}{\beta^2} \times \dfrac{1}{\gamma^{-2}}$$

$$= \dfrac{5\gamma^2}{\alpha\beta^2}\,J$$

This is the required value of energy in the new system of units.

EXERCISES

Multiple Choice Questions

1. $[ML^{-1}T^{-2}]$ is the dimensional formula of
   (A) Force

(B) Coefficient of friction

(C) Modulus of elasticity

(D) Energy.

2. 10^5 Fermi is equal to

(A) 1 meter

(B) 100 micron

(C) 1 Angstrom

(D) 1 mm

3. rad / sec is the unit of

(A) Angular displacement

(B) Angular velocity

(C) Angular acceleration

(D) Angular momentum

4. What is the unit for measuring the amplitude of a sound?

A. **Decibel**
B. Coulomb
C. Hum
D. Cycles

5. The displacement of particle moving along x-axis with respect to time is x=at+bt2-ct3. The dimension of c is

(A) LT^{-2}

(B) T^{-3}

(C) LT^{-3}

(D) T^{-3}

Short Answer Questions

1. Define Physics.

2. What do you mean by physical quantity?

3. Differentiate between fundamental and derived unit.

4. Write full form of the following system of unit

(i) CGS (ii) FPS (iii) MKS

5. Write definition of Dimensions.

6. What is the suitable unit for measuring distance between sun and earth?

7. Write the dimensional formula of the following physical quantity -

(i) Momentum (ii) Power (iii) Surface Tension (iv) Strain

8. What is the principle of Homogeneity of Dimensions?

9. Write the S.I & C.G.S units of the following physical quantities-

(a) Force (b) Work

10. What are the uses of dimensions?

Long Answer Questions

1. Check the correctness of the relation ? = h /mv; where ? is wavelength, h- Planck's constant, m is mass of the particle and v - velocity of the particle.

2. Explain different types of system of units.

3. Check the correctness of the following relation by using method of dimensions

(i) $v = u + at$

(ii) $F = mv^2 / r$

(iii) $v^2 - u^2 = 2as$

4. What are the limitations of Dimensional analysis?

5. Convert an acceleration of 100 m/s2 into km/hr.

Chapter-2: Force and Motion

Unit 2: Force and Motion

Force, Momentum, Conservation of linear momentum, its applications such as recoil of gun, numerical problems rockets (concept only), Impulse and impulsive force.

Circular motion, definition of angular displacement, angular velocity, angular acceleration, frequency, time period, relation between linear and angular velocity, linear acceleration and angular acceleration (related numerical), concept of Centripetal and centrifugal forces with examples (No derivation, only formula) banking of roads and bending of cyclist, concept and formula and numerical problems.

Force and Motion

2.1 Scalar Quantities:

Scalar quantities are those quantities which are having only magnitude but no direction.

Examples: Mass, length, density, volume, energy, temperature, electric charge, current, electric potential etc.

2.2 Vector Quantities:

Vector quantities are those quantities which are having both magnitude as well as direction.

Examples: Displacement, velocity, acceleration, force, electric intensity, magnetic intensity etc.

Representation of Vector: $\vec{A}$ vector is represented by a straight line with an arrow head. Here, the length of the line represents the magnitude and arrow head gives the direction of vector.

Magnitude 5 cm

Types of Vectors

1. **Negative Vectors:** The negative of a vector is defined as another vector having same magnitude but opposite in direction.

   i.e., any vector $\vec{A}$ and its negative vector $[-\vec{A}]$ are as shown.

2. **Equal Vector:** Two or more vectors are said to be equal, if they have same magnitude and direction. If $\vec{A}$ and $\vec{B}$ are two equal vectors then A=B

3. **Unit Vector:** A vector divided by its magnitude is called a unit vector. It has a magnitude one unit and direction same as the direction of given vector. It is denoted by $\hat{A}$. Therefore $\hat{A} = \vec{A}\big/{|A|}$

4. **Collinear Vectors:** Two or more vectors having equal or unequal magnitudes, but having same direction are called collinear vectors.

5. **Zero Vector:** A vector having zero magnitude and arbitrary direction (be not fixed) is called zero vector. It is denoted by $\hat{0}$.

2.3 Addition of Vectors

(i) Triangle law of vector addition.

If two vectors can be represented in magnitude and direction by the two sides of a triangle taken in the same order, then the resultant is represented in magnitude and direction, by third side of the triangle taken in the opposite order.

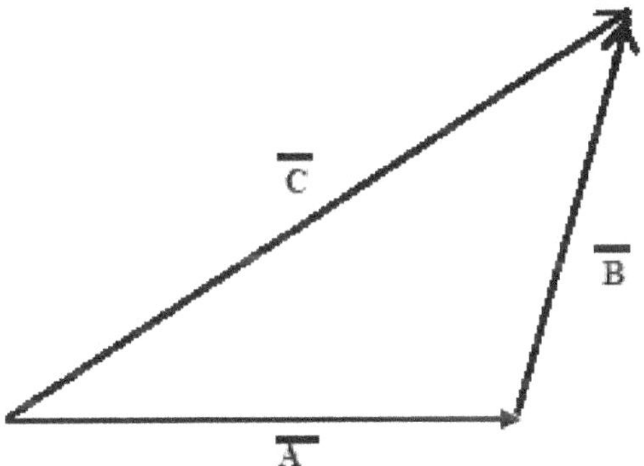

Magnitude of the resultant is given by C = √ (?² + ?² + 2?? ??? ?)

And direction of the resultant is given by ??? ? = ? ??? ?/ (? + ? ??? ?)

(ii) Parallelogram law of vectors:

It states that if two vectors, acting simultaneously at a point, can have represented both in magnitude and direction by the two adjacent sides of a parallelogram, the resultant is represented by the diagonal of the parallelogram passing through that point.

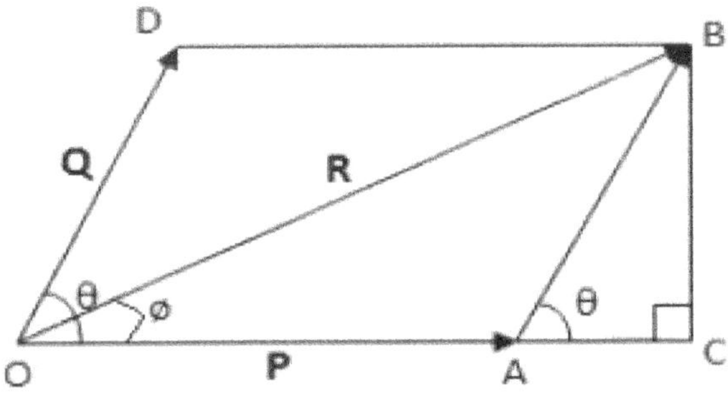

Magnitude of the resultant is given by ?=√ (?²+?²+2??????)

And direction of the resultant is given by ???φ=?????/ (?+?????)

2.4 Multiplication of Vectors

(i) Scalar (or dot) Product: It is defined as the product of magnitude of two vectors and the cosine of the smaller angle between them. The resultant is scalar. The dot product of vectors A and B is defined as

$$\vec{A}.\vec{B} = A\,B\,\cos\theta$$

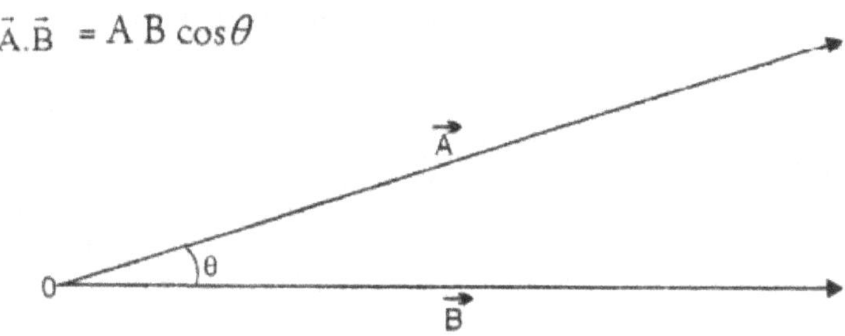

(ii) Vector (or Cross) Product: It is defined as a vector having a magnitude equal to the product of the magnitudes of the two vectors and the sine of the angle between them and is in the direction perpendicular to the plane containing the two vectors.

Thus, the vector product of two vectors A and B is equal to

$$\vec{A} \times \vec{B} = AB\,\sin\theta\;\hat{n}$$

2.5 Definition of distance, displacement, speed, velocity, acceleration

Distance: How much ground an object has covered during it motion. Distance is a scalar quantity. SI unit is meter.

Displacement: The shortest distance between the two points is called displacement. It is a vector quantity.

SI unit is meter.

Dimension formula: [L]

Speed: The rate of change of distance is called speed. Speed is a scalar quantity.

Unit: m/s.

Linear Velocity: The time rate of change of displacement.

Units of Velocity: ms-1

Dimension formula = $[M^0L^1T^{-1}]$

Acceleration: The change in velocity per unit time. i.e. the time rate of change of velocity.

?=?h???? ?? ????????/ ????

If the velocity increases with time, the acceleration 'a' is positive. If the velocity decreases with time, the acceleration 'a' is negative. Negative acceleration is also known as retardation.

Units of Acceleration:

C.G.S. unit is cm/s^2 (cms^{-2}) and the SI unit is m/s^2 (ms^{-2}).

Dimension formula = $[M^0L^1T^{-2}]$

2.6 *Force and its units, concept of resolution of force*

Force: Force is an agent that produces acceleration in the body on which it acts.

Or it is a push or pull which change or tends to change the position of the body at rest or in uniform motion.

Force is a vector quantity as it has both direction and magnitude.

For example,

i. To move a football, we have to exert a push e., kick on the football
ii. To stop football or a body moving with same velocity, we have to apply push in a direction opposite to the direction of the body.

SI unit is Newton.

Dimension formula: $[MLT^{-2}]$

Resolution of a Force

The phenomenon of breaking a given force into two or more forces in different directions is known as 'resolution of force'. The forces obtained on splitting the given force are called components of the given force.

If these are at right angles to each other, then these components are called rectangular components.

Let a force F be represented by a line OP. Let OB (or Fx) is component of F along x-axis and OC (or Fy) is component along y-axis (Fig. 2.5).

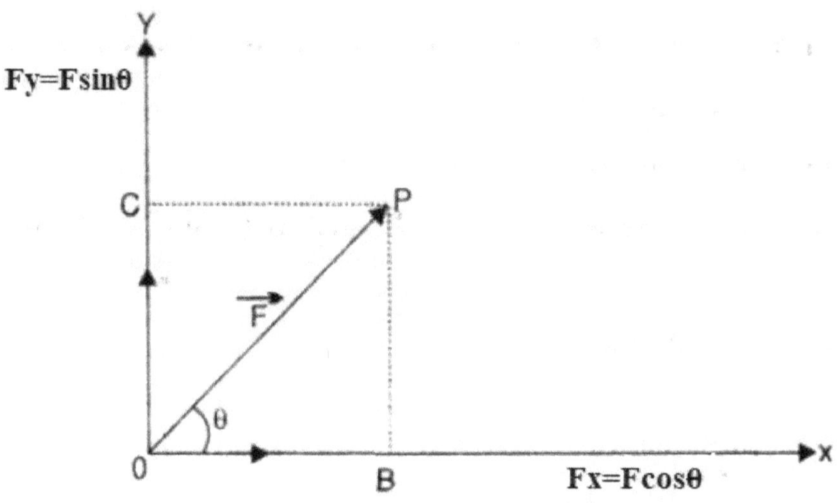

Let force F makes an angle θ with x-axis.

$$\text{In } \Delta \text{ OPB}$$
$$\sin? = ??/??$$
$$PB = OP \sin?$$
$$Fy = F \sin?$$
$$\cos? = ??/??$$
$$OB = OP \cos?$$
$$Fx = F \cos?$$

Vector $\vec{F} = \vec{F_x} + \vec{F_y}$, Therefore Resultant: $F = \sqrt{F_x^2 + F_y^2}$

2.7 Newton's laws of motion

Sir Isaac Newton gave three fundamental laws. These laws are called Newton's laws of motion.

Newton's First Law:

It states that everybody continues in its state of rest or of uniform motion in a straight line until some external force is applied on it.

For example, the book lying on a table will not move at its own. It does not change its position from the state of rest until no external force is applied on it.

Newton's Second law:

The rate of change of momentum of a body is directly proportional to the applied force and the change takes place in the direction of force applied.

Or

Acceleration produced in a body is directly proportional to force applied.

Let a body of mass m moving with a velocity u. Let a force F be applied so that its velocity changes from u to v in t second.

Initial momentum p_1= mu

Final momentum after time t second p_2= mv

Total change in momentum (p_2-p_1) = mv-mu= m (v-u).

Thus, the rate of change of momentum will be $\Delta p/t$= (?–?)/?

From Newton's second law ?$\propto$?(?–?)/?

But (? – ?)/?= ?h???? ?? ????????/ ???? = Acceleration (a)

Hence, we have F$\propto$ **ma**

Or **F = k ma**

Where k is constant of proportionality, for convenience let k = 1.

Then **F = ma**

Units of force:

One **dyne** is that much force which produces an acceleration of $1cm/s^2$ in a mass of 1 gm.

1 dyne = 1gm x 1 cm/s^2

= 1gm.cm s^{-2}

One **Newton** is that much force which produces an acceleration of 1 m/s2 in a mass of 1kg.

Using F = ma

1N = 1kg x 1m/s^2

or = 1kgm/s^2

IN =1000gm×100 cm/s^2 = 10^5 dyne

Newton's Third law:

To every action there is an equal and opposite reaction or action and reaction are equal and opposite.

When a body exerts a force on another body, the other body also exerts an equal force on the first, in opposite direction.

From Newton's third law these forces always occur in pairs.

$$F_{AB} \text{ (force on A by B)} = -F_{BA} \text{ (force on B by A)}$$

2.8 Linear Momentum, Conservation of Momentum, Impulse

Linear Momentum (p):

The quantity of motion contained in the body is linear momentum. It is given by product of mass and the velocity of the body. It is a vector and its direction is the same as the direction of the velocity.

Let m is mass and v is the velocity of a body at some instant, then momentum is given by

$$p = mv$$

Example, a fast-moving cricket ball has more momentum in it than a slow moving one. But a slow-moving heavy roller has more momentum than a fast cricket ball.

Units of momentum:

The SI unit is kg m/s i.e. $kg.ms^{-1}$.

Dimension formula = $[M^1L^1T^{-1}]$.

Conservation of Momentum

If external force acting on a system of bodies is zero then the total linear momentum of a system always remains constant.

i.e. If F=0

Thus,$=??/??=0$

Hence, p (momentum) is constant.

Recoil Velocity of the Gun:

When a bullet is fired with a gun the bullet moves in forward direction and gun is recoiled/pushed backwards. Let m = mass of bullet, u= velocity of bullet, M= mass of gun, V= velocity of gun

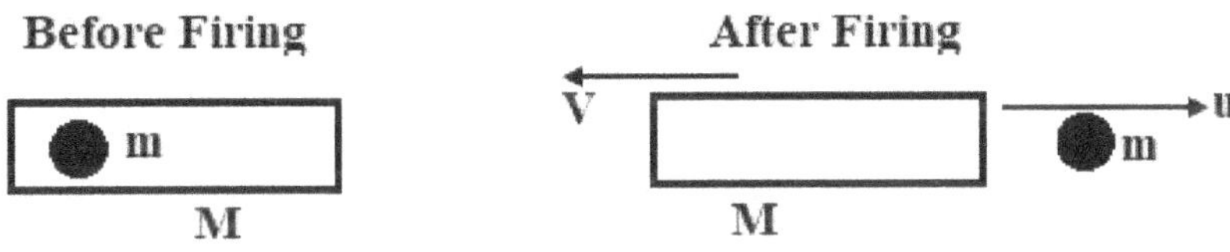

The gun and bullet form an isolated system so the total momentum of gun and bullet before firing

$$P \text{ (initial)} = 0$$

Total momentum of gun and bullet after firing

$$P \text{ (final)} = m.u + M.v$$

Using law of conservation of momentum

$$P \text{ (initial)} = P \text{ (final)}$$

$$0 = m.u + M.v$$

$$M.v = -m.u$$

$$? = -??/?$$

This is the expression for recoil velocity of gun.

Here negative sign shows that motion of the gun is in opposite direction to that of the bullet. Also, velocity of gun is inversely proportional to its mass. Lesser the mass, larger will be the recoil velocity of the gun.

Impulse

Impulse is defined as the total change in momentum produced by the impulsive force.

OR

Impulse may be defined as the product of force and time and is equal to the total change in momentum of the body.

$$F.t = p_2 - p_1 = \text{total change in momentum}$$

Example. A kick given to a football or blow made with hammer.

2.9 Circular Motion

Circular Motion: The motion of a body in a circle of fixed radius is called circular motion.

For example, the motion of a stone tied to a string when whirled in the air is a circular motion.

Angular Displacement: The angle described by a body moving in a circle is called angular displacement. Consider a body moves in a circle, starting from A to B so that $\angle BOA$ is called angular displacement SI unit of angular displacement is radian (rad.)

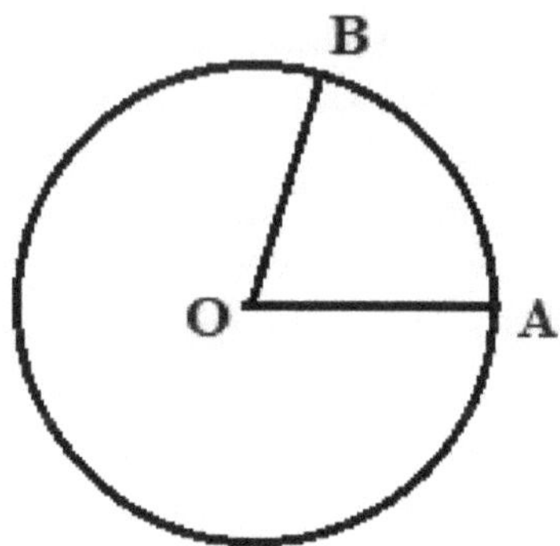

Angular Velocity: Angular velocity of a body moving in a circle is the rate of change of angular displacement with time. It is denoted by ω (omega)

If θ is the angular displacement in time t then ? = ?/?

SI unit of angular velocity is rad/s.

Time Period: Time taken by a body moving in a circle to complete one cycle is called time period. It is denoted by T

Frequency (n): The number of cycles completed by a body is called frequency. It is reciprocal of time period

$$? = 1/?$$

Angular Acceleration: The time rate of change of angular velocity of a body. It is denoted by α. Let angular velocity of a body moving in a circle change from $\omega1$ to $\omega2$ in time t, then

$$? = (?1-?2) / ?$$

SI unit of '?' is rad/s^2

Relationship between linear and angular velocity

Consider a body moving in a circle of radius r Let it start from A and reaches to B after time t, so that ∠BOA = θ.

Now ????? = ??? / ?????? ?

= ??/??=?/?

?=??

Divide both side by time (t) ?/?=??/?

Here ?/?=? is linear velocity

And ?/?=? is angular velocity

Hence ?=??

2.10 Centripetal and Centrifugal forces

Centripetal Force:

The force acting along the radius towards the centre of circle to keep a body moving with uniform speed in a circular path is called centripetal force. It is denoted by F_C.

$$??=??^2/?$$

For example, a stone tied at one end of a string whose other end is held in hand, when round in the air, the centripetal force is supplied by the tension in the string.

Centrifugal Force:

A body moving in circle with uniform speed experience a force in a direction away from the centre of the circle. This force is called centrifugal force.

For example, cream is separated from milk by using centrifugal force. When milk is rotated in cream separator, cream particles in the milk being lighter, and experience less centrifugal force.

2.11 Application of centripetal force in banking of roads

Banking of Roads: While travelling on a road, you must have noticed that, the outer edge of circular road is slightly raised above as compared to the inner edge of road. This is called banking of roads (fig 2.8).

Angle of Banking: The angle through which the outer edge of circular road is raised above the inner edge of circular roads is called angle of banking

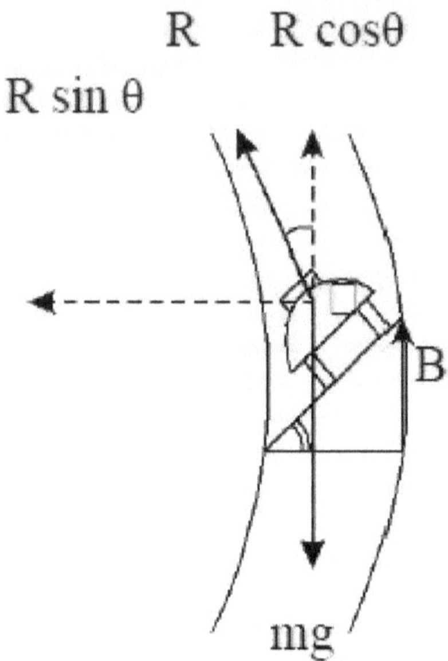

Application of centripetal force in banking of roads

Let m = mass of vehicle, r=radius of circular road, v=uniform speed (velocity) of vehicle, θ = angle of banking

At the body two forces act.

(i) Weight (mg) of vehicle vertically downwards.

(ii) Normal reaction (R).

R makes an angle θ and divides the forces into two components

(i) Rsinθ towards the centre

(ii) Rcosθ vertically upwards and balance by weight of (mg) vehicle

Rsinθ provides the necessary centripetal force $(??^2/?)$

$$R \, Sin\theta = ??^2 / ? \, ----- (1)$$

$$And \; R \, Cos\theta = mg \, ----- (2)$$

Divide equation 1 by 2

$$????? / ????? = (??^2 / ?) / ??$$

$$???? = ?^2 / ??$$

$$? = ???^{-1} (?^2 / ??)$$

θ giving the expression ofangle of banking.

-------------- X ----------------

2.12 Important Questions & Answers

Q1. Name the factor on which the coefficient of friction depends.

Ans: The coefficient of friction will mainly depend on two factors, which are as follows:

The materials of the surfaces in contact.

The characteristics of the surfaces.

Q2. What provides the centripetal force to a car taking a turn on a level road?

Ans: Centripetal force is provided by the frictional contact between the tyres and the road.

Q3. Why does a swimmer push the water backwards?

Ans: From Newton's 3rd Law of Motion, we know that "when one body exerts a force on the other body, the first body experiences a force equivalent in magnitude in the opposite direction of the force exerted". As a result, the swimmer pushes water backward with his hands in order to swim ahead.

Q4. Action and reaction forces do not balance each other. Why?

Ans: Because a force of action and response always operates on two separate bodies, action and reaction do not balance each other.

Q5. The two ends of a spring-balance are pulled by a force of 10 kg each. What will be the reading of the balance?

Ans: As the spring balancing is based on the tension in the spring, it gauges weight. Now, if both ends are pulled by a 10kg weight, the tension is 10kg, and the reading will be 10kg.

Q6. A lift is an acceleration upward. Will the apparent weight of a person inside the lift increase, decrease, or remain the same relative to its real weight? What happens if the lift is going at a uniform speed?

Ans: There will be an increase in perceived weight. The apparent weight will stay the same as the true weight if the lift moves at a constant pace.

Q7. Why is it desirable to hold a gun tight to one's shoulder when it is being fired?

Ans. Because the gun recoils after being fired, it must be held softly on the shoulder. Because the gun and the shoulder are combined into one mass system, the back kick is reduced. When shooting, a gunman must keep his weapon securely against his shoulder.

Q8. Justify that friction is a self-adjusting force.

Ans: Friction is a self-adjusting force that changes in magnitude from zero to maximum to limit friction.

Q9. A bird is sitting on the floor of a wire cage, and the cage is in the hand of a boy. The bird starts flying in the cage. Will the boy experience any change in the weight of the cage?

Ans: When the bird begins to fly within the cage, the weight of the bird is no longer felt since the air inside is in direct touch with ambient air, making the cage look lighter.

Q10. Why does a cyclist lean to one side, while going along a curve? In what direction does he lean?

Ans: A cyclist leans while riding along a curve because a component of the ground's natural response supplies him with the centripetal force he needs to turn. He must lean inward from his vertical posture, towards the circular path's centre.

Q11. Explain why passengers are thrown forward from their seats when a speeding bus stops suddenly.

Ans: When a fast bus comes to a complete stop, the bottom half of the body in touch with the seat comes to a complete halt, while the upper section of the passengers' bodies prefer to retain their uniform motion. As a result, the passengers are pushed forward.

Q12. How does road banking reduce tyre wear and tear?

Ans: When a curving road is not banked, friction between the tyres and the road provides centripetal force.

Friction must be increased, resulting in wear and tear. When the curving road is banked, however, a component of the ground's natural response supplies the necessary centripetal force, reducing tyre wear and tear.

Q13. A force is being applied to a body, but it causes no acceleration. What possibilities might be considered to explain the observation?

Ans: (1) If the force is a deforming force, no acceleration is produced.

(2) Internal force is incapable of causing acceleration.

EXERCISES

Multiple Choice Questions

1. What is the maximum possible number of components of a vector can have

(A) 2

(B) 3

(C) 4

(D) Any number

2. Which of the following operations with two vectors can result in a scalar

(A) Addition

(B) Subtraction

(C) Multiplication

(D) None of these

3. The acceleration of the particle performing uniform circular motion is

(A) ω^2/r

(B) zero

(C) vr

(D) v^2/r

4. Centripetal force always acts at 90 degrees to the velocity, and away from the centre of the circle.

(A) True

(B) False

(C) Can't predict

(D) None of these

5. Railway tracks are banked at the curves so that the necessary centripetal force may be obtained from the horizontal component of the reaction on the train

(A) True

(B) False

(C) Can't predict

(D) None of these

6. Which of the following is called a fictitious force?

(A) Gravitational force

(B) Frictional force

(C) Centrifugal force

(D) Centripetal force

7. At which place of the earth, the centripetal force is maximum

(A) At the earth surface

(B) At the equator

(C) At the North Pole

(D) At the South Pole

8. The angle through which the outer edge is raised above the inner edge is called

(A) Angle of inclination

(B) Angle of repose

(C) Angle of banking

(D) Angle of declination

9. A model aeroplane fastened to a post by a fine thread is flying in a horizontal circle. Suddenly the thread breaks. What direction will the aeroplane fly?

(A) In a circular path, as before

(B) Directly to the centre of the circle

(C) In a straight line at a tangent

(D) Directly to the centre of the circle.

10. A force which acts for a small time and also varies with time is called:

(A) Electrostatic force

(B) Electromagnetic force

(C) Impulsive force

(D) Centripetal force

Short Answer Type Questions

1. State and explain laws of vector addition.

2. What do you understand by resolution of a vector?

3. How is impulse related to linear momentum?

4. What do you mean by circular motion? Give examples?

5. What do you mean by banking of roads?

3. What are scalar and vector quantities? Give examples?

4. Define resolution and composition of forces.

5. What is impulse?

6. Why does a gun recoil when a bullet is fired?

7. Differentiate between centripetal and centrifugal forces?

8. An artificial satellite takes 90 minutes to complete its revolution around the earth. Calculate the angular speed of satellite. [Ans. 2700 rad/sec]

9. At what maximum speed a racing car can transverse an unbanked curve of 30 m radius? The co-efficient of friction between types and road is

0.6. [Ans. 47.8]

10. Justify the statement that Newton's second law is the real law of motion.

11. Define Force. Give its units.

12. Define Triangle law of vector addition.

13. State parallelogram law of vector addition.

Long Answer Type Questions

1. Explain Newton's Law of Motion.

2. Explain Banking of Roads.

3. What is conservation of momentum?

4. Derive relationship between linear and angular velocity.

5. Derive a relation between linear acceleration and angular acceleration.

Chapter 3: Work, Power and Energy

Unit 3: Work, Power and Energy

Work: Concept and units, examples of zero work, positive and negative work

Friction: concept, types, laws of limiting friction, coefficient of friction, reducing friction and its engineering applications, Work done in moving an object on rough inclined plane.

Energy and its units, kinetic energy and potential energy, Conservation of mechanical energy for freely falling bodies (simple numerical problems), transformation of energy (examples only).

Power and its units, power and work relationship, calculation of power (numerical problems).

Work, Power and Energy

3.1 Work

Work is said to be done when the force applied on a body displaces it through certain distance in direction of applied force.

$$\text{Work} = \text{Force} \times \text{Displacement}$$

In vector form, it is written as; $\vec{F}.\vec{S} = FScos\theta$

It is measured as the product of the magnitude of force and the distance covered by the body in the direction of the force. It is a scalar quantity.

Unit: SI unit of work is joule (J). In CGS system, unit of work is erg.

$1\ J = 10^7$ ergs

Dimension of work = $[M^1L^2T^{-2}]$

3.2 Energy

Energy of a body is defined as the capacity of the body to do the work. Like work, energy is also a scalar quantity.

Unit: SI system - Joule, CGS system - erg

Dimensional Formula: $[ML^2\ T^{-2}]$.

Transformation of Energy

The energy change from one form to another is called transformation of energy.

For an example.

• In a heat engine, heat energy changes into mechanical energy

• In an electric bulb, the electric energy changes into light energy.

• In an electric heater, the electric energy changes into heat energy.

• In a fan, the electric energy changes into mechanical energy which rotates the fan.

• In the sun, mass changes into radiant energy.

• In an electric motor, the electric energy is converted into mechanical energy.

• In burning of coal, oil etc., chemical energy changes into heat and light energy.

• In a dam, potential energy of water changes into kinetic energy, then K.E rotates the turbine which produces the electric energy.

• In an electric bell, electric energy changes into sound energy.

• In a generator, mechanical energy is converted into the electric energy.

3.3 Kinetic Energy (K.E):

Energy possessed by the body by virtue of its motions is called kinetic energy.

For example; (i) running water (ii) Wind energy; work on the K.E. of air (iii) Moving bullet.

Expression for Kinetic Energy

Consider F is the force acting on the body at rest (i.e., $u = 0$), then it moves in the direction of force to distance (s).

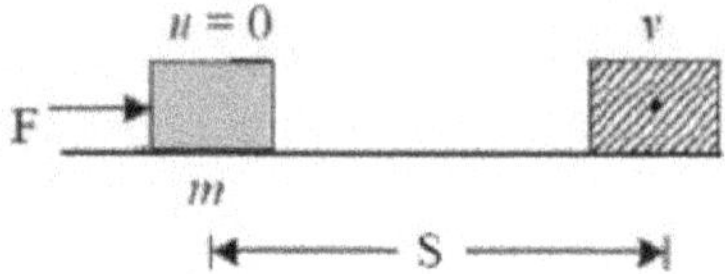

Let v be the final velocity.

Using relation

$$v^2 - u^2 = 2aS$$

$$a = \frac{v^2 - u^2}{2S}$$

$$a = \frac{v^2 - 0}{2S} = \frac{v^2}{2S}$$

Now,

$$W = \vec{F}.\vec{S}$$

$$W = ma.S = m\frac{v^2}{2S}.S = \frac{1}{2}mv^2$$

This work done is stored in the body as kinetic energy. So kinetic energy possessed by the body is (K.E.)

$$K.E = \frac{1}{2}mv^2$$

3.3 Potential Energy (P.E):

Potential Energy (P.E.): Energy possessed by the body by virtue of its position is called potential energy. Example

(i) Water stored in a dam

(ii) Mango hanging on the branch of a tree

Expression for Potential Energy (P.E)

It is defined as the energy possessed by the body by virtue of its position above the surface of earth.

W=FxS

Workdone = Force × height

= mg × h = mgh

This work done is stored in the form of gravitational potential energy. Hence Potential energy **P.E=mgh.**

3.4 Law of Conservation of Energy

Energy can neither be created nor be destroyed but can be converted from one form to another.

3.5 *Conservation of Mechanical Energy of a Free Falling Body*

Let us consider K.E., P.E. and total energy of a body of mass m falling freely under gravity from a height h from the surface of ground.

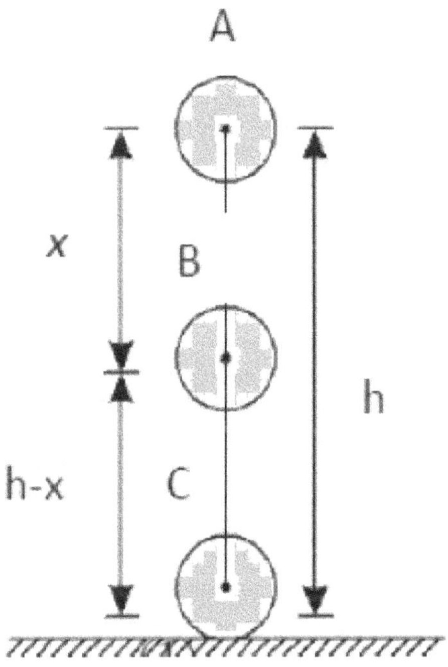

According to Fig. 3.2

At position A:

$$\text{Initial velocity } (u) = 0$$

$$K.E = \frac{1}{2} mv^2$$

$$P.E. = mgh$$

$$\text{Total Energy} = K.E + P.E = 0 + mgh = mgh \dots\dots\dots(1)$$

At position B:

$$\text{Potential energy} = mg(h - x)$$

$$\text{Velocity at point B} = u$$

$$\text{From equation of motion K.E.} = \frac{1}{2} mu^2$$

$$As\ V^2 - U^2 = 2aS$$
$$Hence\ u^2 - 0 = 2gx$$
$$Or\ u^2 = 2gx$$

Putting this value we get, KE= ½ m(2gx) = mgx

Total Energy =K.E + P.E = mgx + mg(h – x) = mgh ....(2)

At position C

$$Potential\ energy = 0\ (as\ h = 0)$$
$$Velocity\ at\ Point\ B = v$$
$$From\ equation\ of\ motion\ K.E. = ½\ mv^2$$
$$As\ V^2 - U^2 = 2aS$$
$$Hence\ v^2 - 0 = 2gh$$
$$Or\ v^2 = 2gx$$

Putting this value we get KE = ½ m(2gh) = mgh

Total Energy = K.E + P.E = mgh + 0 = mgh ....(3)

From equations (1), (2) and (3), it is clear that total mechanical energy of freely falling body at all the positions is same and hence remain conserved.

3.6 Power

Power is defined as the rate at which work is done by a force. The work done per unit time is also called power.

If a body do work W in time t, then power is

$$P=W/t$$

Units of Power: SI unit of power is watt (W)

Power is said to be 1 W, if 1 J work is done in 1 s.

$$1W=1J/1sec$$

Bigger units of power are:

Kilowatt (KW) =10^3W

Megawatt (MW) =10^6 W

Horse power (hp) = 74^6 W

Dimension of power = $[M^1 L^2 T^{-3}]$

3.7 Solved Numerical Problems:

1. What work is done in dragging a block 10 m horizontally when a 50 N force is applied by a rope making an angle of 30° with the ground?

Sol. Here, F = 50 N, S = 10 m, θ = 30

W = FS Cos θ

W = 50 × 10 × Cos 30° = 50x10x $\sqrt{3}/2$= 612.4 J

1. A man weighing 50 kg supports a body of 25 kg on head. What is the work done when he moves a distance of 20 m.

Sol. Total mass = 50 + 25 = 75 kg , θ = 90°, Distance = 20 m
W = FS × 0 (as Cos 90° = 0)
W = 0
Thus, work done is zero.

1. A man weighing 50 kg carries a load of 10 kg on his head. Find the work done when he goes (i) 15 m vertically up (ii) 15 m on a levelled path on the ground.

Sol. Mass of the man, m_1= 50 kg
Mass carried by a man, m_2 = 10 kg
Total mass M = $m_1 + m_2$ = 50 + 10 = 60 kg.
When the man goes vertically up,
Height through which he rises, h = 15 m
Hence Workdone W =Mgh = 60 × 9.8 × 15 = 8820 J
When the man goes on a levelled path on the ground.
W= FS Cos θ As θ =90°, therefore, Cos 90°= 0
Hence Workdone W= F×S×0 =0

4. A spring extended by 20 mm possesses a P.E. of 10 J. What will be P.E., if the extension of spring becomes 30 mm?

Sol. h = 20 mm = 20 × 10^{-3}m, g = 9.8 m/s^{-2}, m = ?
P.E =mgh = 10J
i.e., m × 9.8 × 20 × 10^{-3} = 10 J
m =51.02 Kg
When extension is 30 mm i.e., 30 × 10^{-3} m, then
P.E =mgh = 51.02 × 9.8×3 × 10^{-3}= 15.0 J

5. A man weighing 65 kg lifts a mass of 45 kg to the top of a building 10 meters high in 12second. Find;

(i) Total work done by him. (ii) The power developed by him.

Sol. Mass of the man, m1= 65 kg, Mass lifted m2= 45 kg, Height through which raised h = 10 m

Time taken t = 12 seconds.

(i) Total work done by the man, W = mgh = 110 × 9.81 × 10 = 10791.0J

(ii) Power developed P=W/t = 10791/ 12 = 899.25 W

------------ X ------------

3.8 Important Questions & Answers

Q.1 Does work done depend upon the velocity of the body.
Ans. No.

Q.2 State the law of conservation of energy.

Ans. It states that energy can neither be created nor destroyed. It can only change its form.

Q.3 In a tug-of-war one team gives way to the other. What work is being done and by whom ?
Ans. The winning team does work. The work is equal to the product of the resultant force and the displacement undergone by the losing team.

Q.4 What will cause greater change in kinetic energy of a body? Changing its mass or changing its velocity?
Ans. Changing its velocity.

Q.5 List two essential conditions for work to be done.
Ans. (i) A force must act and (ii) There should be displacement in the body.

Q.6 When is 1 joule of work said to be done?
Ans. When a force of 1 newton acting on a body displaces it in its own direction.

Q.7 What is the SI unit of work done and power?
Ans. Joule and Watt.

Q.8 What is power? What is its SI unit?
Ans. It is defined as the rate of doing work. Its unit is watt.

Q.9 Find the energy in kWh consumed in 10 hours by a machine of power 500 W.
Ans. W = P x t = 500 x 10 = 5000 Wh

Q.10. When is work said to be done against the force of gravity?

Ans. When a body lifted the work is done against the force of gravity.

Q.11 Write an expression for the work done in lifting a body of mass 'm' through a vertical height 'h'.

Ans. Work done W = mgh, where g is acceleration due to gravity.

Q.12 When a book is lifted from a table, against which force work is done?

Ans. Work is done against the force of gravity.

Q.13 Will work be done by a man who pushes a wall?

Ans. No.

Q.14 What is the work done when the force acting on the body and the displacement produced in the body are at right angles to each other?

Ans. Zero.

Q.15 Is it possible that some force is acting on a body but still the work done is zero?

Ans. Yes, when force acts at an angle of 90° with the displacement.

Q.16 What is the work done on a body moving in a circular path?

Ans. Zero, because force and displacement are perpendicular to each other.

Q.17 Does every change in energy of the body involve work?

Ans. Yes.

Q.18 What is the work done in the situation shown below?

Ans. Zero.

Q.19 A body performs no work. Does it imply that the body possesses no energy?

Ans. When a body does not perform any work, it never implies that the body has no energy. The body may have energy but still does not perform any work, e.g., a book placed on a table has potential energy but is not performing any work.

Q.20 What is the SI unit of energy?

Ans. The SI unit of energy is joule.

Q.21 Does a body at rest possess any kinetic energy?

Ans. No.

Q.22 What will happen to the kinetic energy of a body if its mass is doubled?

Ans. Its kinetic energy will be doubled.

Q.23 What will happen to the kinetic energy of a body if its velocity is halved?

Ans. The kinetic energy of the body will become one-fourth.

Q.24 By how much will the speed of a body, of fixed mass, increase if its kinetic energy becomes four times its initial kinetic energy?

Ans. The speed is doubled.

Q. 25 Can a body possess energy even if it is not in motion?

Ans. Yes, it can possess potential energy.

Q.26 Define potential energy.

Ans. It is defined as the energy possessed by a body by virtue of its position or change in shape.

Q.27 Name the energy possessed by a stretched rubber band lying on the table.

Answer. Potential energy.

Q.28 Give the SI unit of potential energy.

Ans. The SI unit of potential energy is joule.

Q.29 What do you mean by trans- formation of energy?

Ans. It is the change of energy from one form of energy into another form of energy.

Q.30 Can energy be destroyed? Can energy be created?

Ans. No,

Q.31 A cell converts one form of energy into another. Name the two forms.

Ans. It converts chemical energy into electrical energy.

Q.32 Name one unit of power bigger than watt.

Ans. A unit bigger than watt is kilowatt.

Q.33 When an arrow is shot from its bow, it has kinetic energy. From where does it get the kinetic energy?

Ans. A stretched bow possesses potential energy on account of a change in its shape. To shoot an arrow; the bow is released. The potential energy of the bow is converted into the kinetic energy of the arrow.

Q.34 What are the various energy transformations that occur when you are riding a bicycle?

Ans. The chemical energy of the food changes into heat and then to muscular energy. On paddling, the muscular energy changes into mechanical energy.

Q.35 Does the transfer of energy take place when you push a huge rock with all your might and fail to move it? Where is the energy you spend going?

Answer. Energy transfer does not take place as no displacement takes place in the direction of applied force; the energy spent is used to overcome inertia of rest of the rock.

Q.36 An object thrown at a certain angle to the ground moves in a curved path and falls back to the ground. The initial and the final points of the path of the object lie on the same horizontal line. What is the work done by the force of gravity on the object ? [SAll-2011]

Ans. Since the body returns to a point which is on the same horizontal line through the point of projection, no displacement has taken place against the force of gravity; therefore, no work is done by the force due to gravity.

Q.37 A battery lights a bulb. Describe the energy changes involved in the process.

Ans. Within the electric cell of the battery the chemical energy changes into electrical energy. The electric energy on flowing through the filament of the bulb, first changes into heat energy and then into the light energy.

Q.38 A mass of 10 kg is at a point A on a table. It is moved to a point B. If the line joining A and B is horizontal, what is the work done on the object by the gravitational force? Explain your answer.

Ans. The work done is zero. This is because the gravitational force and displacement are perpendicular to each other.

Q.39 The potential energy of a freely falling object decreases progressively. Does this violate the law of conservation of energy? Why?

Ans. It does not violate the law of conservation of energy. Whatever, is the decrease in PE due to loss of height, same is the increase in the KE due to increase in velocity of the body.

EXERCISES

Multiple Choice Questions

1. Which of the following is not correct for the condition for work not to be done:

    (A) Force and displacement are perpendicular to each other

    (B) Force and displacement are at 180 degrees with each other

    (C) Displacement is zero, though force is non-zero

    (D) Force is zero

2. There are two bodies X and Y with equal kinetic energy but different masses m and 4m respectively. The ratio of their linear momentum is-

(A) 1:2

(B) 4:1

(C) 1:√2

(D) 1:4

3. Which of the following statements is false:

(A) Kinetic energy is positive

(B) Potential energy is positive

(C) Kinetic energy is negative

(D) Potential energy is negative

4. How should the force applied on a body be varied with velocity to keep the power of force constant?

(A) Force should be inversely proportional to the square root of the velocity of the body

(B) Force should be inversely proportional to the velocity of the body

(C) Force should be directly proportional to the velocity of the body

(D) Force should not be varied. It should remain constant with the velocity

5. When does the potential energy of a spring increase?

(A) Only when spring is stretched

(B) Only when spring is compressed

(C) When spring is neither stretched nor compressed

(D) When spring is compressed or stretched

6. Which of the following force is non-conservative?

(A) Restoring force of spring

(B) Force between two stationary masses

(C) Force between two stationary charges

(D) Human push or pull

7. You are in a lift moving from the 3rd floor to the 12th floor, through a height H. If the elevator moves at a constant speed without stopping, what is the work performed on you by the elevator? Take your body mass as M.

(A) MgH

(B) Mg

(C) -MgH

(D) -Mg

8. Which of the following is not a kind of potential energy?

(A) Gravitational potential energy

(B) Magnetic potential energy

(C) Electrostatic potential energy

(D) Nuclear potential energy

Short Answer Type Questions

1. Define the terms energy, potential energy and kinetic energy.

2. Define potential energy, Derive expression for gravitational potential energy.

3. Define work and write its unit.

4. Define the term power and write its unit.

5. State and prove principle of conservation of energy.

6. Define power. Give it S.I unit.

7. What is transformation of energy?

8. A person walking on a horizontal road with a load on his head does not work. Explain.

9. State kinetic energy. Write expression for kinetic energy of a body of mass m moving at a speed u.

10. Define potential energy of body. Give expression for it.

11. Give some examples of transformation of energy.

12. Define power. Give its units and dimensions.

Long Answer Type Questions

1. Explain the law of conservation of energy for free falling body, show that mechanical energy remains same.

2. What is meant by positive work, negative work and zero work? Illustrate your answer with two examples of each type.

3. What are conservative and non-conservative forces, explain with examples. Mention some of their properties.

4. What is meant by power and energy? Give their units.

5. Explain meaning of kinetic energy with examples. Obtain an expression for kinetic energy of body moving uniformly?

Chapter 4: Rotational Motion

Unit 4: Rotational Motion

Translational and rotational motion with examples, Definition of torque and angular momentum and their relation, Conservation of angular momentum (quantitative) and its applications.

Moment of inertia and its physical significance, radius of gyration for rigid body, Theorems of parallel and perpendicular axes (statements only), Moment of inertia of rod, disc, ring and sphere (hollow and solid); (Formulae only). Simple numerical problems.

Rotational Motion

4.1 Rotational Motion

The rotation of a body about fixed axis is called Rotational motion. For example,

(i) Motion of a wheel about its axis (ii) rotation of earth about its axis.

4.2 Torque and Angular Momentum

Torque (τ)

It is measured by the product of magnitude of force and perpendicular distance of the line of action of force from the axis of rotation.

It is denoted by τ, $\tau = F \times r$

Where F is force and r is perpendicular distance.

Unit: Newton (N)

Dimension Formula: $[M^1 L^2 T^{-2}]$

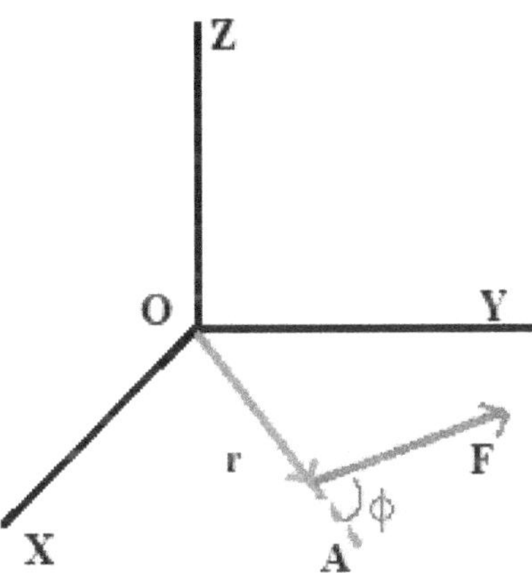

Angular Momentum (L)

Angular momentum of a rotating body about its axis of rotation is the algebraic sum of the linear momentum of its particles about the axis. It is denoted by L.

L = Momentum × perpendicular distance

L=$p \times r$

$$\text{or } L = mvr$$

Unit: Kg m^2/sec

Dimensional Formula = $[ML^2T^{-1}]$

4.3 Conservation of Angular Momentum

Law of Conservation of Angular Momentum

When no external torque acts on a system of particles, then the total angular momentum of the system remains always a constant.

Let I be moment of inertia and ω the angular velocity, then angular momentum is given as

$$L = I\omega$$

Also the torque is given by

$$\tau = dL/dt$$

If no external torque is present on the body i.e., $\tau = 0$

Hence, $dL/dt = 0$

Which means L is constant (as derivative of constant quantity is zero). Hence, if no external torque acts on system, the total angular momentum remains conserved.

Examples:

(i) An ice skater who brings in her arms while spinning spins faster. Her moment of inertia is dropping (reducing the moment of arm) so her angular velocity increases to keep the angular momentum constant

(ii) Springboard diver stretches his body in between his journey.

4.4 *Moment of Inertia and its Physical Significance*

Moment of Inertia

Moment of Inertia of a rotating body about an axis is defined as the sum of the product of the mass of various particles constituting the body and square of respective perpendicular distance of different particles of the body from the axis of rotation.

Expression for the Moment of Inertia:

Let us consider a rigid body of mass M having n number of particles revolving about any axis. Let m1, m2, m3 ..., mn be the masses of particles at distance r1, r2, r3... rn from the axis of rotation respectively (Fig. 4.2).

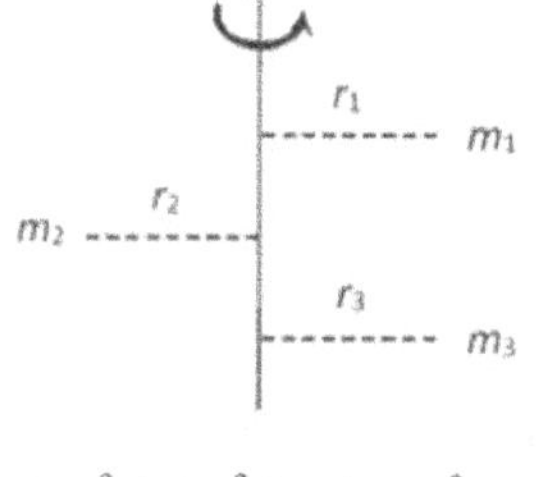

Moment of Inertia of whole body $I = m_1 r_1^2 + m_2 r_2^2 + \cdots + m_n r_n^2$

$$I = \sum_{i=1}^{n} m_i r_i^2$$

Physical Significance of Moment of Inertia

It is totally analogous to the concept of inertial mass. Moment of inertia plays the same role in rotational motion as that of mass in translational motion. In rotational motion, a body, which is free to rotate about a given axis, opposes any change in state of rotation. Moment of Inertia of a body depends on the distribution of mass in a body with respect to the axis of rotation.

4.5 Radius of Gyration

It may be defined as the distance of a point from the axis of rotation at which whole mass of the body is supposed to be concentrated, so that moment of inertia about the axis remains the same. It is denoted by K

If the mass of the body is M, the moment of inertia (I) of the body in terms of radius of gyration is given as,

$$I = MK^2$$

Expression for Radius of Gyration

Let m1, m2, m3 ..., mn be the masses of particles at distance r1, r2, r3... rn from the axis of rotation respectively (Fig. 4.3).

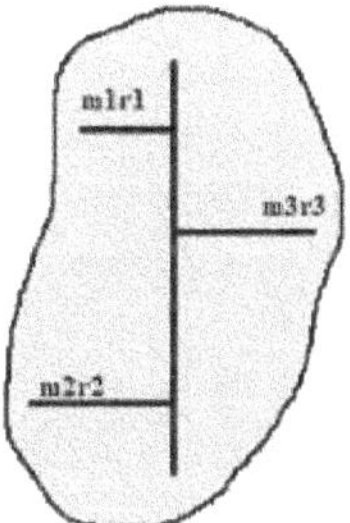

Moment of Inertia of whole body $I = m_1 r_1^2 + m_2 r_2^2 + \cdots + m_n r_n^2$

If mass of all particles is taken same, then $I = m(r_1^2 + r_2^2 + \cdots + r_n^2)$

Multiply and divide the equation by n (number of particle) and M=m×n, is total mass of body

$$I = \frac{mn(r_1^2 + r_2^2 + \cdots + r_n^2)}{n}$$

$$I = \frac{M(r_1^2 + r_2^2 + \cdots + r_n^2)}{n}$$

$$MK^2 = \frac{M(r_1^2 + r_2^2 + \cdots + r_n^2)}{n}$$

$$K^2 = \frac{(r_1^2 + r_2^2 + \cdots + r_n^2)}{n}$$

$$K = \sqrt{\frac{(r_1^2 + r_2^2 + \cdots + r_n^2)}{n}}$$

Thus, radius of gyration may also be defined as the root mean square (r.m.s.) distance of particles from the axis of rotation. Unit: SI unit of radius of gyration is meter.

4.6 Parallel Axis Theorem

The parallel axis theorem states that the moment of inertia of a body about an axis parallel to the body passing through its centre is equal to the sum of the moment of inertia of the body about the axis passing through the centre and the product of the mass of the body times the square of the distance of between the two axes.

Parallel axis theorem statement can be expressed as follows:

$$I = Ic + Mh^2$$

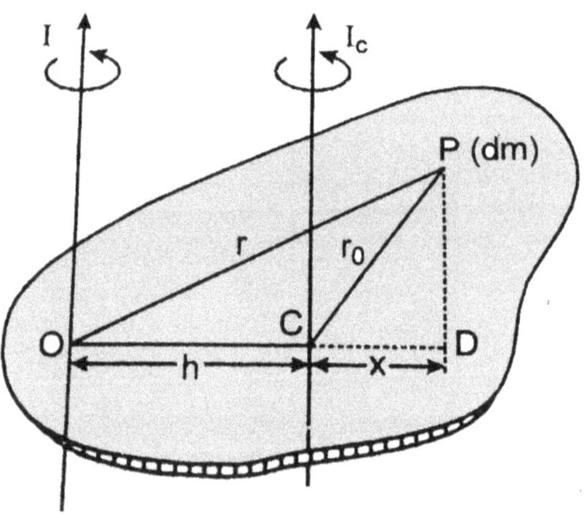

4.7 Perpendicular Axis Theorem

The perpendicular axis theorem states that for any plane body, the moment of inertia about any of its axes which are perpendicular to the plane is equal to the sum of the moment of inertia about any two perpendicular axes in the plane of the body which intersect the first axis in the plane.

Perpendicular axis theorem is used when the body is symmetric in shape about two out of the three axes. If the moment of inertia about two of the axes are known the moment of inertia about the third axis can be found using the expression:

$$Ia = Ib + Ic$$

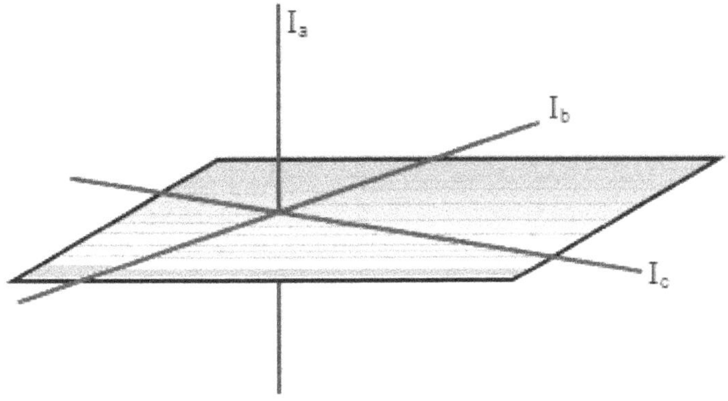

4.8 Moment of inertia of rod, disc, ring and sphere

Object	Drawing	Moment of Inertia
Disk (rotated about center)		$\frac{1}{2}MR^2$
Ring (rotated about center)		MR^2
Rod or plank (rotated about center)		$\frac{1}{12}ML^2$
Rod or plank (rotated about end)		$\frac{1}{3}ML^2$
Sphere		$\frac{2}{5}MR^2$
Satellite	R	MR^2

Object	M.I	Object	M.I
Hollow Cylinder	$I = Mr^2$	Solid Cylinder	$I = \dfrac{Mr^2}{2}$
Hollow Sphere	$I = \dfrac{2Mr^2}{3}$	Solid Sphere	$I = \dfrac{2Mr^2}{5}$

4.9 Solved Numerical Problems

1. What torque will produce an acceleration of 2 rad/s^2 in a body if moment of inertia is 500 kg m^2?

Sol. Here, I= 500 kg m^2, α= 2 rad/s2

$$\text{Now, torque } \tau = I \times \alpha$$
$$= 500 \text{ kg m}^2 \times 2 \text{ rad/s}^2 = 1000 \text{ kg m}^2 s^{-2}$$
$$= 1000 \text{ Nm or J}$$

2. An engine is rotating at the rate of 1500 rev. per minute. Find its angular velocity.

Sol. Here, Revolution per minute of engine, N= 1500

$$\text{Angular velocity } \omega = 2\pi N$$
$$\omega = 2 \times 22/7 \times 1500/60$$
$$\omega = 157.1 \text{ rad/s}$$

3. How large a torque is needed to accelerate a wheel, for which I = 2 kg m^2, from rest to30 r.p.s in 20 seconds?

Sol. Here, Moment of inertia, I= 2 kg m^2, R.P.S after 20 sec, n = 30

$$\text{Initial velocity, } \omega1 = 0$$
$$\text{Final velocity, } \omega2 = 2 \times \pi \times 30 = 188.4 \text{ rad/s.}$$
$$\text{Angular acceleration} = (\omega2 - \omega1)/t = (1.88.4-0)/20 = 9.43 \text{ rad/s}^2.$$
$$\text{Now, torque, } \tau = I \times \alpha$$
$$= 2 \text{ kg m}^2 \times 9.43 \text{ rad/s}^2 = 18.86 \text{ Nm or J}$$

4. If a point on the rim of wheel 4 m in diameter has a linear velocity of 16 m/ s, find the angular velocity of wheel in rad/sec.

Sol. Radius of wheel (R) = Diameter/2 = 4/2 = 2m

$$\text{From the relation v=r } \omega$$
$$\omega = v/r = 8 \text{ rad/s.}$$
$$\text{Angular velocity of wheel is 8 rad/s.}$$

------------- X --------------

4.10 Important Question & Answers

Q1. What is rotational motion? Give an example.

Ans. Rotational motion is a type of motion in which the body follows a circular path. An example is the car wheel.

Q2. What is the reason for rotational motion?

Ans. The torque or rotational analogue force is a reason for rotational motion. When torque is applied to the system of the particle about to its axis, it gives a twist, which is the reason for rotational motion.

Q3. Is circular motion the same as rotational motion? Explain.

Ans. Circular motion: It is a motion of the body around a fixed point. In this case, a fixed point lies outside the body. Here the centripetal force is the reason for the circular motion.

Rotational motion: In the case of rotational motion, the fixed point lies inside the body. Rotational motion is due to the torque acting on the system of the particles.

Q4. Explain how centrifugal force acts in the washing machine?

Ans. A washing machine is basically a spinning top device; thus, when the machine rotates, the centrifugal force balances itself from both sides. When the force exerted by one side of the machine passes through the centre of the machine to act on the other side, a centrifugal force transits into a centripetal force. Therefore, it can be considered as an example of both centripetal and centrifugal force as it totally hangs on its relationship with the centre of the machine.

Q5. Why centrifugal force is called a pseudo force?

A force which arises from gravitational, electromagnetic or nuclear interaction between matters is called a real force. The centrifugal force does not arises due to any of these interactions. Therefore, it is not a real force. The centrifugal force in the non-inertial frame of reference of a particle in circular motion is the effect of the acceleration of the frame of reference with respect to an inertial frame of reference. Therefore, it is called a pseudo or fictitious force.

Q6. When a cat can land on its feet after a fall, which property of Physics is being used by her?

Ans. If the cat can land on its feet after a fall, she is using the principle of conservation of angular momentum.

Q7. What are the factors on which the M.I of a body depends?

Ans. The M.I. of a body depends on the following factors-

Position of the axis of the rotation

Mass of the body.

Way of distribution of mass about the axis of rotation.

Q8. Does the C.M of a body necessarily have to lie inside a body?

Ans. No, the C.M of the body in consideration does not necessarily be inside the body itself. I also may lie outside the body. In the case of the semi-circular ring, it is at the center which is outside the ring.

Q9. What is a rigid body?

Ans. A rigid body refers to an object in which the distance between all the constituting particles remains fixed under any influence of external force. Therefore, a rigid body conserves its shape during motion.

Q10. Distinguish between internal and external forces.

Ans. The mutual forces between the particles of a particular system are called internal forces.

The forces exerted by some kind of external source on the particles of the system are to be named external forces.

Q11. Why are spokes fitted in the cycle wheel?

Ans. The cycle wheel is generally constructed in a way that the M.I of the wheel can be increased with minimum possible mass. This can be achieved by using spokes and the M.I is increased to ensure the uniform speed.

Q12 Why cannot a single force balance the torque?

Ans. The effect of torque can be seen to produce angular acceleration and its effect is entirely different from that of the force that causes linear acceleration. Therefore, a single force cannot balance the torque.

EXERCISES

Multiple Choice Questions

1. The radius of gyration of a ring of radius R about an axis through its centre and perpendicular to its plane is

(A) R / √2

(B) R

(C) R / 2

(D) 5 R / √2

2. Two rings have their moment of inertia in the ratio 2:1 and their diameters are in the ratio 2:1. The ratio of their masses will be:

(A) 1:2

(B) 2:1

(C) 1:4

(D) 1:1

3. The moment of inertia of a body is independent of

(A) Choice of axis of rotation

(B) Its mass

(C) Its shape and size

(D) Its angular velocity

4. A ring has greater moment of inertia than a circular disc of same mass and radius, about an axis passing through its centre of mass perpendicular to its plane, because

(A) All mass is at maximum distance from axis

(B) Because the centre of the ring does not lie on it

(C) Because the ring needs greater inertia to bend it

(D) Because the moment produced in the ring is more

5. A person standing on a rotating platform with his hands lowered outstretches his arms. The angular momentum of the person

(A) Become zero

(B) Decreases

(C) Remain constant

(D) Increases

6. Relation between torque and angular momentum is similar to the relation between

(A) Force and linear momentum

(B) Energy and displacement

(C) Acceleration and velocity

(D) Mass and moment of inertia

7. An earth satellite is moving around the earth in a circular orbit. In such case, what is conserved?

(A) Force

(B) Velocity

(C) Angular momentum

(D) Linear momentum

8. When no external Torque acts on a system, what is conserved?

(A) Energy

(B) Force

(C) Angular momentum

(D) Linear momentum

Short Answer Type Question

1. Define torque.

2. What is moment of inertia?

3. What is Radius of gyration?

4. What is rotational inertia or moment of inertia? Give its SI unit.

5. What is radius of gyration and mention its SI units?

6. What do you understand by kinetic energy of rotation with expression?

7. Derive an expression for torque in terms of moment of inertia.

8. Derive the relation between torque and angular momentum.

Long Answer Type Question

1. Derive an expression for angular momentum in terms of moment of inertia.

2. State and prove law of conservation of angular momentum.

3. What is radius of gyration and derive its expression.

4. What is moment of inertia? Derive its expression and what is its physical significance?

Chapter 5: Properties of Matter

Unit 5: Properties of Matter

Elasticity: definition of stress and strain, moduli of elasticity, Hooke's law, significance of stress-strain curve.

Surface tension: Concept, units, cohesive and adhesive forces, angle of contact, Capillary rise (formula only), applications of surface tension, effect of temperature and impurity on surface tension.

Viscosity and coefficient of viscosity: terminal velocity, Stoke's law and effect of temperature on viscosity.

Hydrodynamics: Fluid motion, stream line and turbulent flow, Reynold's number Equation of continuity, Bernoulli's Theorem (only formula and numerical problem) and its applications (mention name only).

Properties of Matter

5.1 Properties of Matter

Elasticity:

It is the property of solid materials to return to their original shape and size after the forces deforming them have been removed.

Deforming Forces:

The forces which bring the change in configuration of the body are called deforming forces.

Restoring Force:

It is a force exerted on a body or a system that tends to move it towards an equilibrium state.

Elastic Body:

It is the body that returns to its original shape after a deformation. Examples are Golf ball, Soccer ball, Rubber band etc.

Plastic Body:

It is the body that do not return to its original shape after a deformation. Examples are Polyethylene (PE), Polypropylene (PP), Polystyrene (PS) and Polyvinyl Chloride (PVC).

5.2 Stress & Strain

Stress: It is defined as the restoring force (F) per unit area (A) of a material. Therefore Strain=F/A

Unit of Stress: N/m^2 in S.I and $dyne/cm^2$ in C.G.S.

Stress is of two types:

1. Normal Stress: If deforming force acts normal to the surface of the body then the stress is normal stress.
2. Tangential Stress: If deforming force acts tangentially to the surface of the body then the stress is tangential stress.

Strain:

It is defined as the ratio of change in configuration to the original configuration, when a deforming force is applied to a body.

The strain is of three types:

1. **Longitudinal strain:** If the deforming force produces a change in length only, the strain produced is called longitudinal strain or tensile strain. It is defined as the ratio of change in length to the original length.

Longitudinal strain = Change in length (ΔL) / original length (L1)

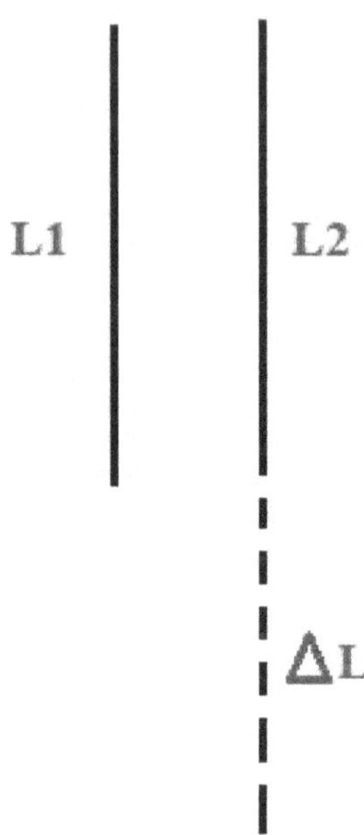

2. Volumetric strain: It is defined as the ratio of the change in volume to the original volume.

Volumetric strain= Change in volume (ΔV) / original volume (V1)

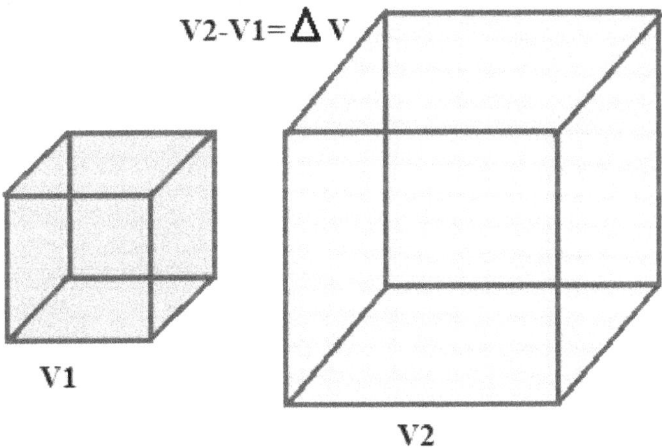

3. Shearing strain: It is defined as the ratio of lateral displacement of a surface under the tangential force to the perpendicular distance between surfaces

Shearing strain= Lateral Displacement / Distance between surfaces

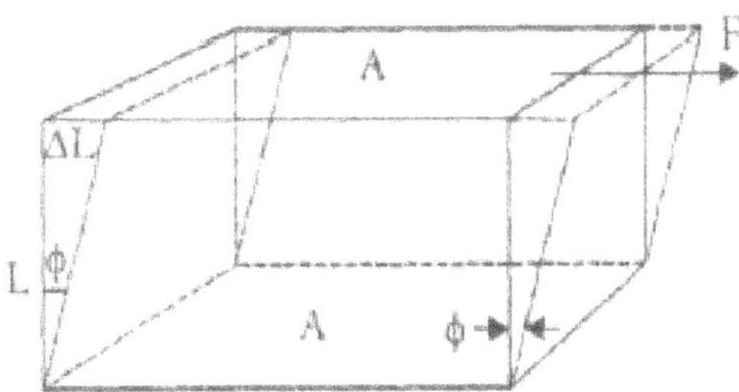

The shearing strain is also defined as the angle in radian through which a plane perpendicular to the fixed surface of a rectangular block gets turned under the effect to tangential force.

Units of strain: Strain is a ratio of two similar physical quantities, it has no units and dimensions.

5.3 Hook's Law

Hook's law: Within elastic limits, the stress and strain are proportional to each other.

$$\text{Thus, Stress} \propto \text{Strain}$$
$$\text{Stress} = E \times \text{Strain}$$

Where E is the proportionality constant and is known as modulus of elasticity.

5.4 Modulus of Elasticity

Modulus of Elasticity: The ratio of stress and strain is called modulus of elasticity.

Different Types of Modulus of Elasticity:

1. **Young's Modulus(Y):** The ratio of normal stress to the longitudinal strain is defined as Young's modulus and is denoted by the symbol Y.

$$Y = (?/?) / (??/?)$$
$$= (?\times?) / (?\times??)$$

Since strain is a dimensionless quantity, the unit of Young's modulus is the same as that of stress i.e., Nm^{-2} or Pascal (Pa).

1. **Bulk Modulus (B):** The ratio of normal (hydraulic) stress to the volumetric strain is called bulk modulus. It is denoted by symbol B.

$$B = (?/?) / (?V/V)$$
$$= (?\times V) / (?\times?V)$$

SI unit of bulk modulus is the same as that of pressure i.e., Nm^{-2} or Pa.

1. **Shear Modulus or Modulus of rigidity (?):** The ratio of shearing stress to the corresponding shearing strain is called the shear modulus of the material and is represented by ?. It is also called the modulus of rigidity.

$$? = \text{Tangential stress} / \text{Shear strain}$$
$$? = (?/?) / \Theta$$

SI unit of shear modulus is Nm^{-2} or Pa.

5.5 Poisson's Ratio

Poisson's ratio is "the ratio of transverse contraction strain to longitudinal extension strain in the direction of the stretching force." Here,

i. Compressive deformation is considered negative
ii. Tensile deformation is considered positive.

Poisson's Ratio (σ) = Transverse strain / Longitudinal strain

Poisson's Effect:

When a material is stretched in one direction, it tends to compress in the direction perpendicular to that of force application and vice versa. The measure of this phenomenon is given in terms of Poisson's ratio.

For example, a rubber band tends to become thinner when stretched.

5.6 Surface Tension

The property of a liquid due to which its free surface behaves like stretched membrane and acquires minimum surface area. It is given by force per unit length.

$$? = ?/?$$

Surface tension allows insects (e.g. water striders), usually denser than water, to float and stride on a water surface.

SI unit is N/m.

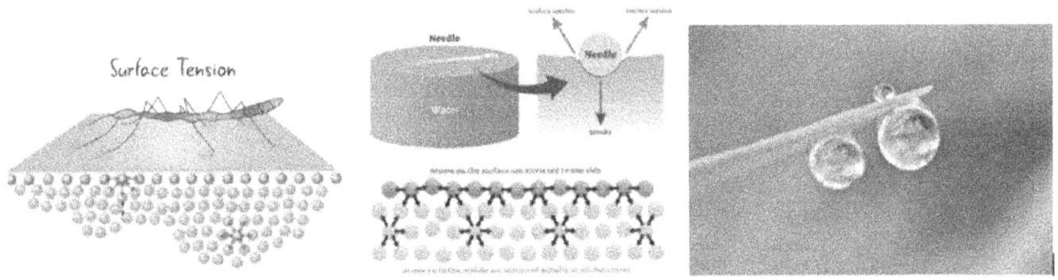

Examples of Surface Tension
There are many examples of surface tension. For example, a water strider is a small insect. It can easily walk on the surface of the water by

the property of surface tension. Some other examples of surface tension are given below:

a. Many insects walk on water's surface without even getting partially submerged.
b. Liquid droplets get their shape through the phenomenon of surface tension.
c. Floating of a needle on the surface of the water.
d. Water bubbles are formed due to the surface tension provided by water in the form of wall tension.
e. The surface tension of water is responsible for bringing down the pores present in the waterproof tents.
f. Cold water washing through the property of surface tension.
g. The tests in clinics for jaundice.
h. The surface tension of water is lowered by cleaning the clothes with detergents and soaps.
a. The surface tension of disinfectants.

5.7 Cohesive Forces, Adhesive Forces:

Cohesive forces:

Cohesive forces are responsible for holding molecules of the same substance together. They arise from intermolecular forces like van der Waals forces and hydrogen bonding. For example, the attraction between water molecules is a cohesive force, leading to water's surface tension.

Example of Cohesion: When water is placed in a container, the water molecules are attracted to each other due to cohesive forces, which helps create the surface tension that allows water to form droplets.

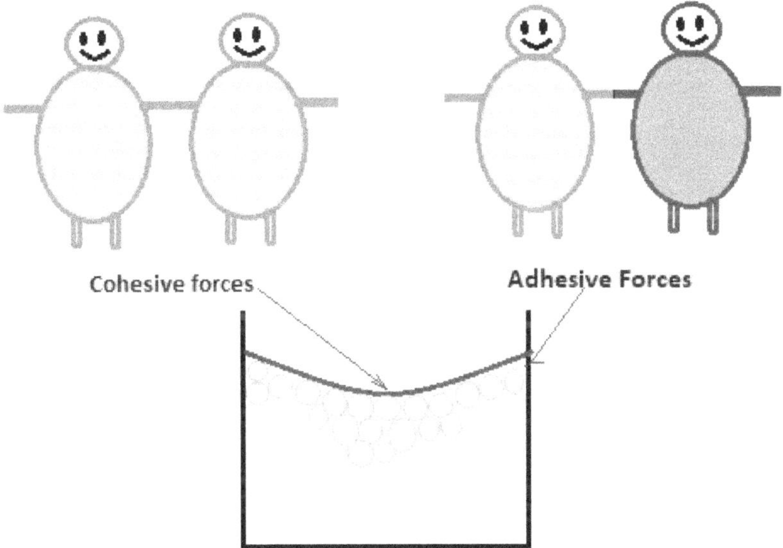

Adhesive Forces:

Adhesive forces act between molecules of different substances, allowing them to stick together. These forces can be electrostatic, mechanical, or due to other intermolecular interactions. An example of adhesion is the attraction between water molecules and the glass molecules of a container, which causes water to stick to the glass.

Example of Adhesion: The attraction between water molecules and the glass molecules of a container is an example of adhesion. This attraction causes the water to stick to the glass, and it can also be seen when water rises up a narrow tube (capillary action).

Impact on Surface Tension and Capillary Action:

Both cohesive and adhesive forces influence surface tension and capillary action. Cohesive forces contribute to the surface tension of liquids, while adhesive forces determine how liquids interact with solid surfaces, affecting whether they will spread or form droplets.

5.8 Angle of Contact:

Angle of Contact: The angle of contact, also known as the contact angle, refers to the angle formed at the interface between a liquid and a solid surface. It is the angle between the tangent line at the point of contact and the solid surface, as measured through the liquid phase. The angle of contact provides information about the wetting behavior of the liquid on the solid surface.

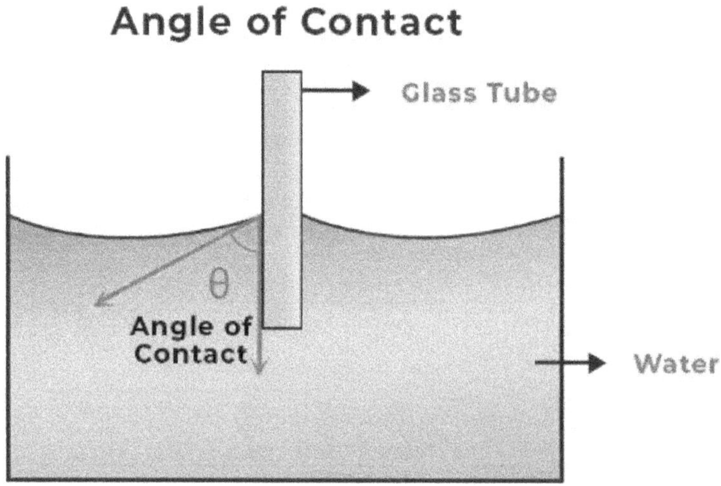

The angle of contact is a crucial parameter that governs the wetting behavior of a liquid on a solid surface. It influences adhesion, surface tension, and capillary phenomena, with wetting angles less than 90 degrees indicating good wetting, angles greater than 90 degrees indicating poor wetting, and angles between 0 and 90 degrees representing partial wetting. Understanding and controlling the angle of contact is essential in various scientific and practical applications involving liquids and solid surfaces. Below is a table summarizing the characteristics of the angle of contact for different wetting behaviors.

5.9 Importance of Angle of Contact

The angle of contact plays a significant role in several important aspects and applications. Here are some key reasons highlighting the importance of the angle of contact:

i. **Wetting and Adhesion:** The angle of contact determines the wetting behavior of a liquid on a solid surface. It indicates the degree of contact and adhesion between the liquid and the surface. Understanding the wetting properties is crucial in processes such as coating, printing, painting, and surface treatment, where the adhesion and spreading of liquids on solid substrates are essential for desired performance and quality.

ii. **Surface Energy and Surface Tension:** The angle of contact is closely related to the surface energy and surface tension of both the liquid and the solid surface. It provides insights into the intermolecular forces and interactions between the two phases. Measurements and control of the angle of contact are valuable in studying surface properties, surface modification techniques, and the behavior of liquids in confined spaces or porous materials.

iii. **Surface Roughness and Topography:** The angle of contact is affected by the surface roughness and topography of the solid surface. It influences the contact area and the resulting wetting behavior. By studying the angle of contact, scientists and engineers can gain insights into the effect of surface roughness on liquid-solid interactions, which is crucial in fields such as tribology, microfluidics, and surface engineering.

iv. **Capillary Action and Fluid Flow:** The angle of contact is involved in capillary action and fluid flow in narrow channels or porous materials. It determines the rise or fall of liquids in capillary tubes and affects the flow rates and dynamics of fluids in microfluidic devices and porous media. Understanding the angle of contact is vital in optimizing fluid flow and controlling capillary phenomena in various scientific, industrial, and biomedical applications.

5.10 Capillary Rise

We can define capillary action as a phenomenon where the ascension of liquids through a tube or cylinder takes place. This primarily occurs due to adhesive and cohesive forces. The liquid is drawn upward due to this interaction between the phenomena. The narrower the tube, the higher will the liquid rise. If any of the two phenomena, i.e., that of surface tension and a ratio between cohesion to adhesion, increase, the rise will also increase. Although, if the density of the liquid increases, the rise of the liquid in the capillary will lessen.

The formula for capillary rise is: $h = (2T\cos\theta) / (r\rho g)$

Where h is the height of the liquid rise, T is the surface tension of the liquid, θ is the contact angle between the liquid and the solid surface, r is the radius of the capillary tube, ρ is the density of the liquid, g is the acceleration due to gravity.

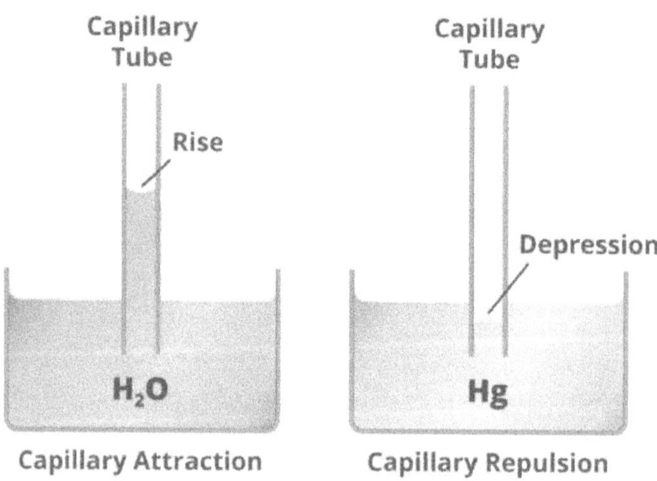

5.11 Applications of Surface Tension

It plays an important role in many applications in our daily life. There are many applications of surface tension in day to day on which daily activities depend. There have been many developments in technologies as well as chemicals to modify surface tension.

a. Soaps and detergents have several uses in everyday life. Everything gets cleaned properly while washing with soaps or detergents. The lower surface tension of water causes the cleansing action of soaps and molecules. This makes it easier for soaps and detergents to act and soak in the areas of clothes or other things that are highly dirty.

b. The surface tension of water decreases by warming the water up. The molecules of water start to move instantly when the water is heated. The intermolecular force of attraction is reduced, and the warmed-up water can be dispersed over the larger surface area.

c. Surface tension plays an important role in physics as well as in chemistry. Hay's test is done for people who have jaundice. This test is highly based on the property of surface tension. It is used to detect the presence of bile salts in urine. Bile salts reduce the surface tension of the droplets of fats in the intestine. This way, fats can easily be broken by enzymes.

d. Sulfur powder is sprinkled on a fresh sample of urine taken for a hay test. Sulfur particles will sink into the bottom of the sample if bile salts are present. This is because bile salts lower the surface tension. This way, the person is tested positive for jaundice.

e. The liquid's ability to flow through the narrow spaces in opposition to gravity forces is known as capillary action. The attraction between glass and water is caused due to force known as adhesion. Due to surface tension, the inside of the glass contracts and starts to rise. This phenomenon can easily be noticed in the liquid molecules present between the hairs of a paintbrush.

f. The liquid present on the top of a tube of mercury is always either convex or concave. This is caused due to surface tension between the cohesive forces and adhesive forces that are present between the walls of the tube. This way, a meniscus is formed. It is widely used to calculate contact angles as well as surface tension.

g. The surface tension of pure water is very high, so the formation of bubbles is very difficult in them. Soap helps to reduce surface tension and hence helps to form bubbles. The surface tension helps to overcome the internal pressure of the bubble.

h. Wine is composed of alcohol and water with some other sugars. Due to the capillary motion of the glass, wine rises from the sides of the glass. The alcohol evaporates due to high vapour pressure. This increases surface tension. This results in droplets on the surface of the wine.

Effect of Temperature on Surface Tension

In general, surface tension decreases when temperature increases and vice versa. This is because cohesive forces decrease with an increase of molecular thermal activity. The influence of the surrounding environment is due to the adhesive action liquid molecules have at the interface.

5.12 Viscosity

The property of liquid due to which it oppose the relative motion between the layers of fluid. It is also known as liquid friction. SI unit of viscosity is Pascal-second (Pa.s) and CGS unit is Poise.

The Coefficient of Viscosity

The force of friction between two layers of fluid having the area in square centimetre and separated by distance will have a velocity is given by:
$f \propto A(dV/dx)$

$$f = \eta A(dV/dx)$$

Here, η is coefficient of viscosity and dV/dx is velocity gradient.

Effect of Temperature on Viscosity

In liquids the source for Viscosity is considered to be atomic bonding. As we understand that, with the increase of temperature the bonds break and make the molecule free to move. So, we can conclude that the viscosity decreases as the temperature increases and vice versa.

In gases, due to the lack of cohesion, the source of viscosity is the collision of molecules. Here, As the temperature increases the viscosity increases and vice versa. This is because the gas molecules utilize the given thermal energy in increasing its kinetic energy that makes them random and therefore resulting in more the number of collisions.

5.13 Stoke's Law

Stoke's Law is a mathematical equation that expresses the settling velocities of the small spherical particles in a fluid medium. The law is derived considering the forces acting on a particular particle as it sinks through the liquid column under the influence of gravity. The force that retards a sphere moving through a viscous fluid is directly proportional to the velocity and the radius of the sphere, and the fluid's viscosity.

Sir George G. Stokes, an English scientist, clearly expressed the viscous drag force F as:

$$F = 6\pi\, \eta r v$$

Where r is the sphere radius, η is the fluid viscosity, and v is the sphere's velocity.

5.14 Terminal Velocity

Terminal velocity is defined as the highest velocity attained by an object falling through a fluid. It is observed when the sum of drag force and buoyancy is equal to the downward gravity force acting on the object. The acceleration of the object is zero as the net force acting on the object is zero.

In fluid mechanics, for an object to attain its terminal velocity, it should have a constant speed against the force exerted by the fluid through which it is moving. The mathematical representation of terminal velocity is:

$$v_t = \sqrt{2mg \big/ \rho A C_d}$$

Where, v_t is the terminal velocity, m is the mass of the falling object, g is the acceleration due to gravity, C_d is the drag coefficient, ? density of the fluid through which the object is falling, and A is the area projected by the object.

5.15 Fluid Motion:

A liquid in motion is called fluid. There are two types of fluid motions; streamline and turbulent.

1. **Streamline Flow:** Flow of a fluid in which its velocity at any point of given cross section is same. Streamline flow, also known as laminar flow, occurs in fluid substances. It is described as a flow where there is no mixing of layers, no turbulence, and no fluctuations in the velocity of the fluid particles, all of them remain constant.

Examples of streamlined flow:

a. Blood flow in veins.
b. Water coming out from a tap.
c. Water fountains placed in gardens.
d. Flow in rivers and canals.
e. Flow in water balloons.
f. Aircraft flying at a constant speed.
g. Viscous fluid like honey.

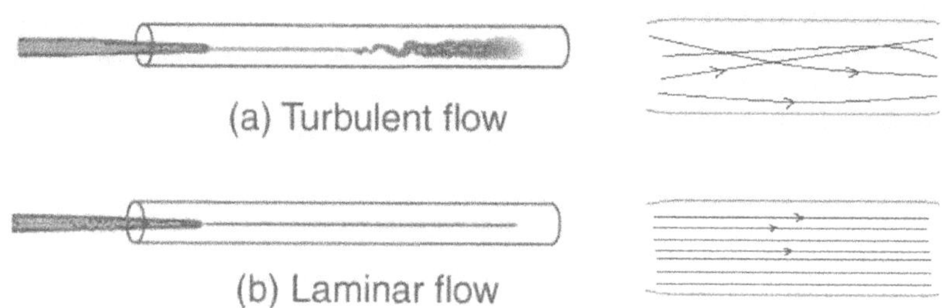

2. **Turbulent flow:** It is type of fluid (gas or liquid) flow in which the speed of the fluid at given cross section is continuously undergoing changes in both magnitude and direction. Turbulent flow is when the fluid layers tend to cross each other and never move parallel to each other, and may meet at some point.

Examples of Turbulent flow:

1. Smoke rising from a cigarette. For the initial few centimetres, the smoke shows features of laminar flow, but after rising, it changes to turbulent flow.
2. Flow over the golf ball.
3. Clear air turbulence is usually experienced during flight take-offs.
4. Oceanic and mixed atmospheric layers, along with strong oceanic currents.
5. Flow of blood through arteries during heart conditions

6. Piers in water as water moves softly around the legs while the river's flow is soft.

5.16 Reynolds Number

Reynolds number is a dimensionless quantity that is used to determine the type of flow pattern as laminar or turbulent while flowing through a pipe. Reynolds number is defined by the ratio of inertial forces to that of viscous forces. It is given by the following relation:

Reynolds number = inertial force / viscous force

If the Reynolds number calculated is high (greater than 2000), then the flow through the pipe is said to be turbulent. If Reynolds number is low (less than 2000), the flow is said to be laminar. Numerically, these are acceptable values, although in general the laminar and turbulent flows are classified according to a range. Laminar flow falls below Reynolds number of 1100 and turbulent falls in a range greater than 2200.

5.17 Equation of Continuity

Continuity equation represents that the product of cross-sectional area of the pipe and the fluid speed at any point along the pipe is always constant. This product is equal to the volume flow per second or simply the flow rate. The continuity equation is given as:

R = A v = constant

Where, R is the volume flow rate, A is the flow area, v is the flow velocity.

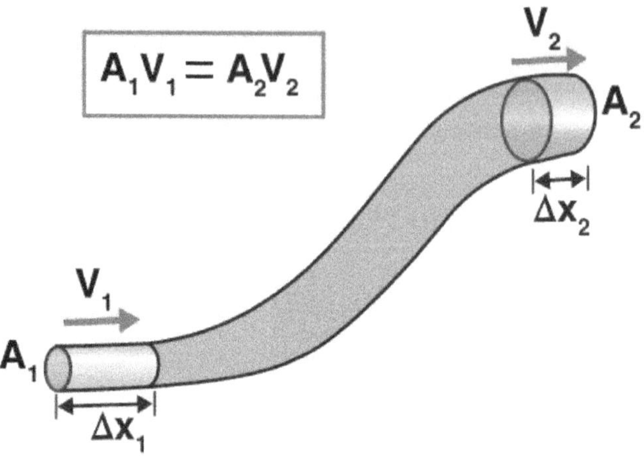

5.18 Bernoulli's Theorem

The total mechanical energy of the moving fluid comprising the gravitational potential energy of elevation, the energy associated with the fluid pressure and the kinetic energy of the fluid motion, remains constant.

The relationship between the pressure of a fluid which flows to its elevation and its velocity is given by an equation called the Bernoulli equation. This equation is based on conservation of energy and their conversion into each other.

The formula of Bernoulli's principle is a relationship between pressure, kinetic energy, and gravitational potential energy of a fluid which is kept inside a container. Bernoulli theorem formula is given as

$$p + 1/2\ \rho \times v^2 + \rho \times g \times h = \text{constant}$$

Here, p = pressure exerted by fluid, p= density of fluid, v = Fluid velocity, g = Acceleration due to gravity, h = height of container

Use of Bernoulli's Principle

Bernoulli's Principle has many applications. Some of the uses of Bernoulli's Principle are given here.

a. Bernoulli's principle is used to examine the unsteady flow which is applicable in the theory of ocean surface waves and acoustics.

b. Working of an aeroplane: The shape of the wings is such that the air passes at a higher speed over the upper surface than the lower surface. The difference in airspeed is calculated using Bernoulli's principle to create a pressure difference.

c. Bernoulli theorem is also used for approximation of parameters such as pressure and velocity of the fluid.

d. Venturi meter is a device which is based on Bernoulli's principle and used for determining the rate of flow of liquid through the pipes.

------------- X --------------

5.19 Important Question & Answers:

Q1. What happens to a rigid body when external forces are applied to it?

Ans. When external forces are exerted on a rigid body, there will be a variation in its length, shape or volume.

Q2. What is the property of a body that allows it to come back to its original shape or size when external forces are removed?

Ans. The property of a body that allows it to come back to its original shape or size when external forces are removed is called elasticity.

Q3. What are elastic stress and strain?

Ans. Elastic stress and strain are the internal force and deformation, respectively, experienced by an elastic body under external forces.

Q4. What happens to internal and external forces when an elastic body is deformed?

Ans. When an elastic body is deformed, internal restoring forces are generated that oppose the external forces.

Q5. What is longitudinal stress?

Ans. Longitudinal stress is stress that is normal to the surface area of the body and causes a change in the length of the body.

Q6. What are the two types of longitudinal stress?

Ans. The two types of longitudinal stress are tensile stress and compressive stress.

Q7. What is tensile stress?

Ans. Tensile stress is longitudinal stress produced due to an increase in the length of the object.

Q8. What is compressive stress?

Ans. Compressive stress is longitudinal stress produced due to the decrease in the length of the object.

Q9. What is volume stress?

Ans. Volume stress is the stress that occurs when equal normal forces are applied to the body, causing a change in the volume of the body.

Q10. Which is more elastic steel or diamond?

Ans. **Diamond is more elastic than steel**

Magnitude of elastic limit is the degree of elasticity of a material. Higher the elastic limit of a material, greater is its degree of elasticity. The elastic limit of diamond is more than that of steel and hence diamond is more elastic than steel.

Q11. Explain why the temperature of a wire under tension will change if it snaps suddenly.

Ans. **The temperature of a wire under tension will change if it snaps suddenly**

During elongation of a wire the work done remains stored as elastic potential energy in the wire. When the wire snaps suddenly, that stored potential energy is transformed into heat energy resulting in increase in temperature.

Q12. Springs are usually made of steel but not of copper. Why?

Ans. **Springs are usually made of steel but not of copper.**

Elasticity of steel is more than that of copper. It means that the elastic limit of steel is greater. Let us consider two springs of the same size, one of steel and another of copper.

An equal tensile force is applied on both springs. On slowly increasing the magnitude of the applied force on the two springs it is seen that, at a certain stage the steel spring still behaves like an elastic body but the copper spring undergoes a permanent deformation. For this reason, springs are usually made of steel but not of copper. Moreover, copper is costlier than steel. However, copper springs may be used where the applied force is not very high.

Q13. In the case of an elastic body which one is more fundamental—stress or strain?

Ans. When an elastic body gets strained under the influence of external forces, a reaction force develops inside the body. This is the source of stress. This stress helps the deformed body to regain its original shape. It means that only when strain is produced in a body, a stress is developed within it.

So, elastic strain is more fundamental than stress.

Q14. Can a steel wire be elongated to twice its initial length by hanging a load from its end?

Ans. By hanging a load from its free end, a steel wire cannot be elongated to twice its initial length. This is because the wire snaps before attaining that elongation, as it crosses its breaking load.

Q15. How does the value of modulus of elasticity change due to increase in temperature?

Ans. In most cases, the value of elastic modulus decreases slightly due to increase in temperature

Q16. Two soap bubbles of unequal sizes are blown at the ends of a capillary tube. Which one will grow at the expense of the other and what does it show?

Ans. The larger will grow at the expense of the smaller. This is due to the fact that excess pressure is inversely proportional to radius and air flows from higher to lower pressure.

Q17. The paints and lubricating oils have low surface tension. Why?

Ans. Paints and lubricating oils with low surface tension can spread over a large surface area.

Q18. An oil drop on a hot cup of soup spreads over when the temperature of the soup falls. Why?

Ans. Since hot water has a lower surface tension than oil, oil drops do not spread over it. Water's surface tension decreases as it cools. At low temperatures, the surface tension of water exceeds that of oil, and thus oil drops begin to spread over it.

Q19. What shape does a liquid take when it weighs nothing? Give reason to support your answer.

Ans. When a liquid has no weight, the only force acting on it is surface tension. The liquid surface tends to occupy the smallest amount of surface area due to surface tension. Because the surface area of a sphere is the smallest for a given volume, the liquid takes on a spherical shape.

Q20. What is the effect of contamination and temperature on the surface tension of a liquid?

Ans. Temperature Effect: As the temperature rises, the surface tension of the liquid decreases. It decreases linearly for small temperature differences. A liquid's surface tension is zero at its boiling point. As a result, the boiling point is referred to as the critical temperature of that liquid. Contaminations effect: If there is dust, grease, oil, or other impurities on the liquid's surface, the surface tension decreases.

21. What is the angle of contact?

Ans. The angle of contact, also known as the contact angle, is the angle formed at the interface between a liquid and a solid surface. It provides information about the wetting behavior of the liquid on the solid surface.

Q22. How does the angle of contact affect adhesion?

Ans. The angle of contact determines the degree of contact and adhesion between a liquid and a solid surface. A smaller angle indicates better wetting and adhesion, while a larger angle suggests poor wetting and reduced adhesion.

Q23. How is the angle of contact related to surface energy?

Ans. The angle of contact is influenced by the surface energy of both the liquid and the solid surface. Lower surface energy of the liquid or higher surface energy of the solid surface leads to smaller contact angles, indicating better wetting and adhesion.

Q24. How does surface roughness affect the angle of contact?

Ans. Surface roughness influences the angle of contact. Smoother surfaces tend to have smaller contact angles, resulting in better wetting, while rougher surfaces can have larger contact angles and reduced wetting due to decreased surface area available for contact.

Q25: Why liquids have a definite volume, but no definite shape?

Ans. It's because intermolecular forces in liquids are strong enough to hold the molecules together, but not strong enough to fix them into definite or concrete locations like they are in solids. As a result, they are fluid but lack a defined shape.

Q26. Name the property due to which a bloating paper can absorb ink.?

Ans. Capillary.

EXERCISES

Multiple Choice Questions

1. Elastic body is the body that returns to its original shape after a ....
A. Restoration
B. Deformation

C. Elongation

D. Acceleration

2. Stress *is* defined as the .... per unit area of a material.

   A. **Force**
   B. Velocity
   C. Distance
   D. Displacement

   3. ....is the ratio of change in dimensions to the original dimensions.

   A. **Strain**
   B. Surface Tension
   C. energy
   D. elasticity

   4. For small deformations the stress and strain are proportional to each other. This is called ....

   (A) Hook's Law

   B. Pascal's Law
   C. Snell's law
   D. Newton's law

   5. Pressure *is* defined as the force per unit .... over the surface of a body.

   A. **Area**
   B. Volume
   C. Line
   D. Energy

   6. A change in the pressure applied to an enclosed incompressible fluid is transmitted undiminished to every portion of the fluid to the walls of its container. It is called.....................

A. Hooks Law
B. **Pascal's Law**
C. Snell's law
D. Newton's law

7. Elasticity is the property of solid materials to return to their original shape and size after the removal of deforming forces.

A. **True**
B. False

8. Restoring force is the force exerted on a body or a system that tends to move it towards an equilibrium state.

A. **True**
B. (B) False

Short *Answer Type Questions*

1. Define Elasticity.
2. What is Viscosity?
3. What is Turbulent Flow?
4. Define Surface Tension.
5. What is Young's Modulus of Elasticity?
6. State and explain Hooks Law.
7. State and explain Pascal's Law.
8. What is the effect of temperature on surface tension?
9. What is the effect of temperature on viscosity?
10. Give any five applications of Surface Tension.
11. What is difference between elastic and plastic bodies?

Long *Answer Type Questions*

1. Explain different kind of modulus of elasticity.

2. What is Surface Tension? Give formula, Units and Applications of Surface Tension.
3. Explain streamline flow, laminar flow and turbulent flow.
4. Explain different types of stress.
5. Explain Young's modulus and its units.

Chapter 6: Heat and Thermometry

Unit 6: Heat and Thermometry

Concept of heat and temperature, basic concepts of measurements of heat and temperature, modes of heats transfer (conduction, convection and radiation with examples), Co-efficient of thermal conductivity simple numerical problems.

Expansion of solids, liquids and gases, coefficient of linear, surface and cubical expansions of solids and relation amongst them, specific heats Cp & Cv of a gas and their relationship (Mention only).

Heat and Thermometry

6.1 Heat and Temperature

Heat

All objects are made of atoms or molecules. These molecules are always in some form of motion (linear, vibrational or rotational) and possess kinetic energy by virtue of their motion. The hotter an object is, faster will be the motion of the molecules inside it and hence more will be its kinetic energy. Heat of an object is the total energy of all the individual molecules of which the given object is made. It is a form of thermal energy. When the object is heated, its thermal energy increases, means its molecules begin to move more violently. Temperature, on the other hand, is a measure of the average heat or thermal energy of the molecules in a substance.

Heat is the form of energy which produces the sensation of warmth or coldness.

Conventionally, heat energy supplied to a body is taken as positive and the heat energy given out by a body is taken to be negative.

The CGS unit of heat is the calorie (cal) – defined as the amount of heat required to raise the temperature of 1g of water through 1°C. The S.I. unit of heat energy is the Joule (J) – defined as the amount of work done when a force of one Newton acts through one meter parallel to itself.

The relationship between two units is: 1 cal = 4.18 J.

Heat on the basis of kinetic theory: According to the kinetic theory, heat of a body is total kinetic energy of all its molecules. If a body have 'n' number of molecule having mass m and velocities v1, v2, v3, --------, vn respectively, then

Total heat energy in the body (H) = Sum of kinetic energy of all molecules

$$H = K \left(\frac{1}{2} mv_1^2 + \frac{1}{2} mv_2^2 + \cdots + \frac{1}{2} mv_n^2 \right)$$

Where K is thermal constant.

When the body is heated, the kinetic energy of each molecule inside it increases due to in their velocity. This results in the increase of total kinetic energy of the body and in turn represents total heat of the body.

Temperature

Temperature is the degree of hotness of the body. It is the average kinetic energy of all the molecules of which the given body is made and is given by the expression;

$$T = \frac{K \left(\frac{1}{2} mv_1^2 + \frac{1}{2} mv_2^2 + \cdots + \frac{1}{2} mv_n^2 \right)}{n}$$

Units of temperature are; Fahrenheit ($^{\circ}$F), Celsius ($^{\circ}$C) and Kelvin (K). Kelvin is the S.I. unit of temperature.

6.2 Difference between Heat and Temperature:

Heat	Temperature
Heat is energy that is transferred from one body to another as the result of a difference in temperature	Temperature is a measure of hotness or coldness
It is total kinetic energy of all the molecules	It is average kinetic energy of all the molecules
It depends on quantity of matter	It does not depend on quantity of matter
It is form of energy (Thermal)	It is measure of energy
S.I. unit is Joule	S.I. unit is Kelvin

6.3 Principles of Measurement of Temperature:

Measurement of temperature depends on the principle that properties (physical/electrical/chemical) of material changes with change in temperature. A device that utilizes a property of matter to measure temperature is known as thermometer. Temperature is a principle parameter that needs to be monitored and controlled in most engineering applications such as heating, cooling, drying and storage. Temperature can be measured via a diverse array of sensors. All of them infer temperature by sensing some change in a physical characteristic; be it a thermal expansion, thermoelectricity, electrical resistance or thermal radiation. There are four basic types of thermometers, each working on a different principle:

1. Mechanical (liquid-in-glass, bimetallic strips, bulb & capillary, pressure type etc.)

2. Thermo-electric (Thermocouples)

3. Thermo-resistive (RTDs and thermistors)

4. Radiative (Infrared and optical pyrometers).

Each produces a different scale of temperature which can be related to one another. Commonly used thermometers are mercury thermometer, platinum resistance thermometer, thermo-electric and pyrometers. Liquid thermometers can measure temperature up to 300°C. Resistance thermometers can go up to 1200°C while thermo-electrics are used for measuring temperature as high as 3000°C. For still higher temperatures pyrometers (very hot furnaces) are used.

6.4 Different Scales of Temperature and their relationship

In general, there are three scales of temperature measurement. The scales are usually defined by two fixed points; temperature at which water freezes and the boiling point of wateras defined at sea level and standard atmospheric pressure.

1. **Fahrenheit Scale:** It was given by physicist Daniel Gabriel Fahrenheit in 1724. It uses the degree Fahrenheit (symbol: °F) as the unit. On this scale freezing point of water is taken as the lower fixed point (32°F) and boiling point of water is taken as upper fixed point (212°F). The interval between two points is divided into 180 equal parts. Each division is 1o F. This scale is used for clinical and meteorological purpose.

2. **Celsius Scale:** This scale was given by Anders Celsius in 1742. The scale was called centigrade scale. However in 1948 it was given the name Celsius to honour Anders Celsius. On this scale freezing point of water is taken as the lower fixed point (marked 0°C) and boiling point of water is taken as upper fixed point (marked 100°C). The interval between two points is divided into 100 equal parts. Each division is 1oC.This scale is used for common scientific, clinical, meteorological and technological work.

3. **Kelvin Scale:** In1954, the Celsius scale was redefined in terms of the absolute zero and the triple point of a specially purified water. This definition also precisely relates the Celsius scale to the Kelvin, which defines the SI base unit of temperature with symbol K. On this scale freezing point of water is taken as the lower fixed point (273K) and boiling point of water is taken as upper fixed point (373K). The interval between two points is divided into 100 equal parts. Each division is 1K. 1oC = 1 K This is the natural scale of temperature also called the absolute temperature scale. Absolute zero is the basis of the Kelvin scale. The scale is based on ideal gas thermometer.

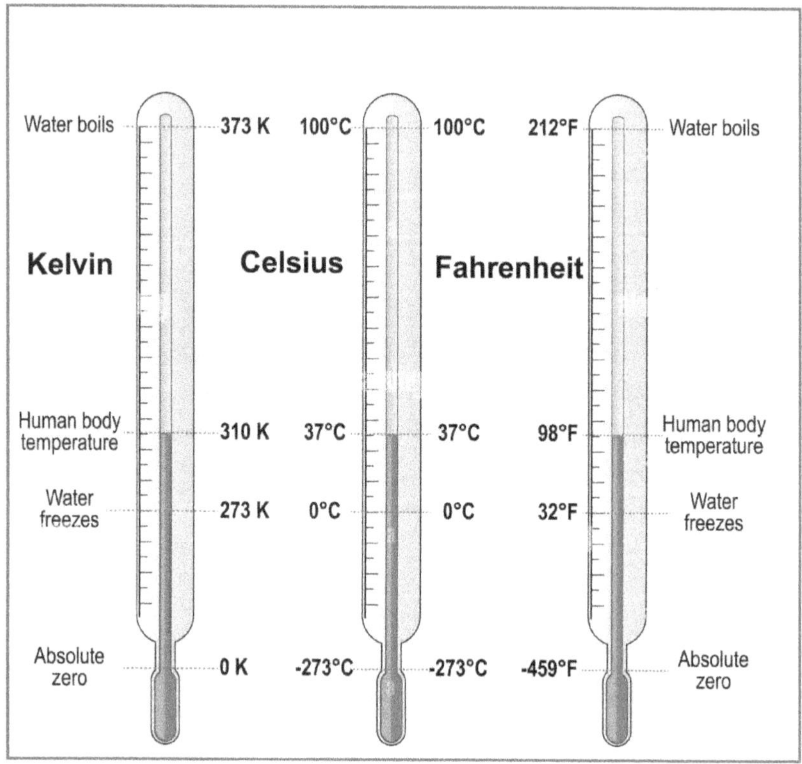

Absolute Zero: Absolute zero is the temperature at which all molecular motions comes to stand still i.e. net kinetic energy becomes zero. It is taken as zero Kelvin (-273° C). At absolute zero temperature, the pressure (or volume) of the gas goes to zero. This may implies that if the temperature is reduced below -273.15°C, the volume becomes negative which is obviously not possible. Hence -273.15°C is the lowest temperature that can be achieved and therefore called the absolute zero of temperature. The interval on the scale is the same as on the Celsius scale (1 K = 1 °C) and two scales can be related as.

$$K = {}^{\circ}C + 273.15$$

Thus on absolute scale of temperature, water freezes at 273.15K and boils at 373.15K.

Triple Point of water: The triple point is that point on a pressure versus temperature graph which corresponds to the equilibrium among three phases of a substance i.e. gas, liquid and solid. Triple point of pure water is at 273.15K. It is unique and occurs at single temperature and single pressure.

6.5 Relation among the Scales of Temperature

Temperature of a body can be converted from one scale to the other.

Let, L = lower reference point (freezing point), H = upper reference point (boiling point), T = temperature read on the given scale.

Now $(T-L) / (H-L)$ = Relative temperature w.r.t. both reference point.

This relative temperature should not change if we are measuring the temperature of a body by using different thermometers.

Let us take a body whose temperature is determined by three different thermometers giving readings in °C, °F and K respectively.

Let $T1 = C$ = Temperature in °C, $L1 = 0°C$ $H1 = 100°C$

$T2 = F$ = Temperature in °F, $L2 = 32°F$ $H2 = 212°F$

$T3 = K$ = Temperature Kelvin, $L3 = 273 K$ $H3 = 373K$

We can write,

$$(T1-L1) / (H1-L1) = (T2-L2) / (H2-L2) = (T3-L3) / (H3-L3)$$
$$(C-0) / (100-0) = (F-32) / (212-32) = (K-273) / (373-273)$$
$$C/100 = (F-32) / 180 = (K-273) / 100$$
$$\mathbf{C/5 = (F-32) / 9 = (K-273) / 5}$$

6.6 Modes of Transfer of Heat

When two bodies having different temperatures are brought close together, the heat flows from body at higher temperature to body at lower temperature. Heat may also flow from one portion of body to another portion because of temperature difference. The process is called transfer of heat. There are three modes by which heat is transferred from one place to another. These are named as conduction, convention and radiations.

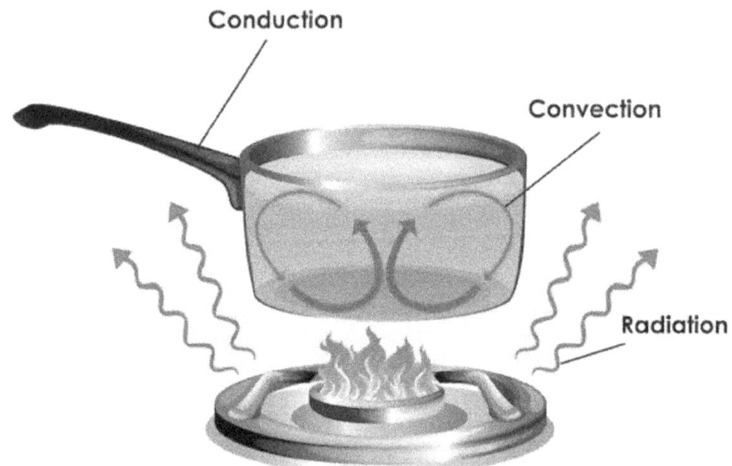

Different Mode of Heat Transfer

a. Conduction:

It is defined as that mode of transfer of heat in which the heat travels from particle to particle in contact, along the direction of fall of temperature without any net displacement of the particles.

If one end of a long metal rod (iron or brass) is heated, after some time other end of rod also become hot. This is due to the transfer of heat energy from hot atoms to the nearby atoms. When two bodies have different temperatures and are brought into contact, they exchange heat energy and tend to equalize the temperature. The bodies are said to be in thermal equilibrium. This is the mode of heat transfer in solids.

Examples are:

1. Touching a hot stove: Heat transfers directly from the stove to your hand through contact.
2. Walking on hot sand: Heat is transferred from the hot sand to your feet through direct contact.
3. Ice cooling your hand: Heat is transferred from your hand to the ice, causing it to melt.

4. Burning your tongue on hot soup: Heat is transferred from the soup to your tongue through direct contact.
5. Holding a hot cup of coffee: Heat is transferred from the cup to your hands.

b. Convection:

The process of transmission of heat in which heat is transferred from one point to another by the physical movement of the heated particles is called convection.

If a liquid in a vessel is heated by placing a burner below the vessel, after some time the top surface of liquid also become warm. This is because the speed of atoms or molecules increases when liquid or gases are heated. The molecule having more kinetic energy rise upward and carry heat with them. Liquids and gases transfer heat by convection. Examples are heating of water, cooling of transformers, heating of rooms by heater etc.

Examples are:

1. Hot air rising above a fire: Hot air expands, becomes less dense, and rises, creating convection currents.
2. Boiling water: As water heats up in a pot, the warmer water rises, and cooler water sinks, causing convection.
3. A hot air balloon rising: Hot air inside the balloon is less dense than the surrounding cooler air, causing it to rise.
4. The effect that causes water in the ocean getting colder as you go deeper: Convection currents cause the water to mix and transfer heat.
5. Steam from a hot shower: Hot water vaporizes and rises, carrying heat with it, which is an example of convection.

c. Radiation:

The process of heat transfer in which heat is transmitted from one place to another without heating the intervening medium is called radiation. Thermal radiations are the energy emitted by a body in the form of radiations on account of its temperature and travel with the velocity of light.

We receive heat from sun by radiation process. All the bodies around us do emit these radiations. These radiations are the electromagnetic waves. The energy contained in radiation is $E = h\nu$, where ν is frequency of waves emitted.

1. Heat from the sun: The sun emits electromagnetic radiation, which heats the Earth.
2. Heat from a light bulb: A light bulb emits electromagnetic radiation, which can be felt as heat.
3. Putting your hand beside a stove burner: You can feel the heat from the burner without touching it, due to radiation.
4. Sunbathing on the beach: The sun's rays transfer heat to your skin through radiation.
5. A microwave heating your food: Microwaves are a form of electromagnetic radiation that heats the food.

Properties of Heat Radiations

a. They do not require a medium for their propagation.
b. Heat radiations travel in straight line.
c. Heat radiations do not heat the intervening medium.
d. Heat radiations are electromagnetic waves.
e. They travel with a velocity 3×10^8 m/s in vacuum.
f. They undergo reflection, refraction, interference, diffraction and polarization.
g. They obey inverse square law.

6.7 Difference between Conduction, Convection and Radiation:

Sr. No.	Feature	Conduction	Convection	Radiation
1	Definition	Transfer of heat through direct contact of particles	Transfer of heat through the movement of fluid (liquid or gas)	Transfer of heat through electromagnetic waves (no medium)
2	Medium	Solids	Liquids and gases	No medium required, occurs in a vacuum or through air
3	Particle Movement	Vibrational motion of particles	Movement of fluid particles (bulk motion)	Electromagnetic waves (no particle movement)
4	Heat Transfer Rate	Generally slower compared to other methods	Faster, especially in fluids	Travels at the speed of light, very fast
5	Examples	Heating one end of a metal rod	Boiling water, heating a room	Sunlight warming the Earth, heat from a fire
6	Dependency on Density Changes	Not affected by changes in the density of the material	Heavily influenced by changes in fluid density and viscosity	Not affected by the medium's density or state
7	Natural Phenomenon	Commonly occurs in solids and some liquids	Frequently observed in liquids and gases	Occurs naturally and is observed in various phenomena
8	Application	Thermal insulation materials, cooking utensils	HVAC systems, natural convection in atmosphere	Solar heating, microwave cooking, thermal imaging, etc.

6.8 Thermal Conductivity

The capacity of a substance to transport heat is referred to as thermal conductivity. For example, wood conducts heat less effectively than metals because of its less structured atomic structure, while metals transmit heat well because of their densely packed atoms and free electrons. On a stove, a plastic container takes longer to heat than a metal pot. Choosing materials for specialized uses, such as insulation or cooking, is made easier with an understanding of heat conductivity.

Coefficient of Thermal Conductivity:

Coefficient of thermal conductivity is the measurement of the ability of a substance to conduct heat. It represents the rate at which heat flows through a unit area of a material with a unit temperature gradient. Materials with a high coefficient of thermal conductivity are conductors, while those with a low coefficient of thermal conductivity are insulators or poor conductors of heat. The formula of coefficient of thermal conductivity is given as k= Q /(A·ΔT·t)

Where Q is the amount of heat transferred through the material (in watts), A is the cross-sectional area through which the heat flows (in square meters), T is the temperature difference across the material (in degrees Celsius or Kelvin), and t is the time over which the heat transfer occurs (in seconds).

Unit of Coefficient of Thermal Conductivity

The SI unit of measurement for thermal conductivity is watts per meter-kelvin (W/mK), i.e., $Wm^{-1}K^{-1}$. It is represented by the symbol k.

This unit indicates the quantity of heat energy (measured in watts) that may per unit temperature differential (measured in kelvin) over a material having a thickness of one meter.

6.9 Factors Affecting Thermal Conductivity

Following factors affect the thermal conductivity of a material:

a. Material Composition: Different materials have varying heat-conduction properties. Heat energy may be easily transferred and carried by electrons in metals such as aluminum and copper, which makes them good heat conductors. Plastics and ceramics, on the other hand, have a lower heat conductivity because they contain less free electrons.

b. Crystal Structure: Thermal conductivity is dependent on the configuration of atoms in a material's crystal lattice. Better in conducting heat than materials with more disordered structures are those with highly ordered structures, like graphite or diamond.

c. Density: Thermal conductivity is influenced by a material's density, or how closely its atoms are packed. Denser materials are often more thermally conductive because they have more atoms accessible for heat transmission.

d. Temperature: Different materials respond differently to temperature in terms of thermal conductivity. Some people experience a gain in thermal conductivity with temperature, whereas others experience a fall. These differences might be caused by modifications in the crystal structure or atomic vibrations.

e. Pressure: When pressure is applied, a material's electrical or crystal structure may change, which may have an impact on the material's thermal conductivity. Pressure has the ability to either enhance or reduce heat conductivity, depending on the substance.

f. Moisture Content: A material's heat conductivity can be affected by impurities or moisture. Adding water to a material can enhance its total thermal conductivity because, in comparison to other liquids, water has a comparatively high thermal conductivity.

6.10 Thermal Expansion

Thermal expansion is the phenomenon observed in solids, liquids, and gases. In this process, an object or body expands on the application of heat (temperature). Thermal expansion defines the tendency of an object to change its dimension either in length, density, area, or volume due to heat. When the substance is heated it increases its kinetic energy.

Thermal expansion is of three types:

- Linear expansion
- Area expansion
- Volume expansion

The relative expansion of the material divided by the change in temperature is known as the coefficient of linear thermal expansion. The coefficient of linear thermal expansion generally varies with temperature.

Linear Expansion

Linear expansion is the change in length due to heat. Linear expansion formula is given as,

$$\Delta L / L_0 = \alpha_L \Delta T$$

Where L_0 = original length, L = expanded length, α_L = length expansion coefficient, ΔT = temperature difference, ΔL = change in length

Volume Expansion

Volume expansion is the change in volume due to temperature. Volume expansion formula is given as

$$\Delta V / V_0 = \alpha_V \Delta T$$

Where V_0 = original volume, V = expanded volume, αv = volume expansion coefficient, ΔT = temperature difference, ΔV = change in volume after expansion

Area Expansion

Area expansion occurs is the change in area due to temperature change. Area expansion formula is given as,

$$\Delta A / A_0 = \alpha_A \Delta T$$

Where A = original area, ΔA = change in the area, α_A = area expansion coefficient, ΔT = temperature difference, A_0 = expanded area.

6.11 Comparative Study of Thermal expansion of Solid, Liquid & Gas:

Thermal expansion is the tendency of a body to change its dimension which are either in length, area, density, or volume due to heat. When a substance is heated the kinetic energy of the substance increases.

Thermal expansion of Solid:

a. The particles of solid are always packed tightly.
b. The gaps between the particles of a solid are very less and therefore the compression of solid is tough.
c. The shape and volume of a solid is fixed.
d. Solid is rigid in nature, hence the particles of solid only vibrate about their mean position and cannot move.
e. Attractive force between the particles of solid is adamant.

Example: solid ice, wood, sugar, rock, etc.

Thermal expansion of Liquid:

a. The particles of liquid are less tightly packed when compared to solids.
b. Liquids have the ability to take the shape of the container in which liquids are kept.
c. The particles of liquid have less space between them to move so the compression liquids are difficult but not as in solid.
d. The Volume of Liquid is fixed but the shape of Liquid is not fixed.
e. Rate of Diffusion in liquids is more as compared to solid.

Example: water, milk, coffee, blood etc.

Thermal expansion of Gas:

a. The particles of gas are far from each other.
b. The force of attraction between the particles of gases is almost negligible and hence they can move independently.
c. The volume and shape of gas are not fixed.
d. The particles of gas have more space between them to move so the compression gases are easy.
e. The rate of diffusion is more as compared to solids and liquids.

Example: air, oxygen, nitrogen, carbon dioxide, etc.

6.12 Specific heat capacities of gases

Heat capacity: If a material of mass m absorbs heat Q, its temperature rises through Δ?

Heat capacity =? / Δ?

Specific heat (C): Heat capacity per unit mass

∴ ???????? h??? = ? = ???? ???????? / ????

C=? / (?·Δ?) (or) ? = ? / (?· θ)

Definition: the specific heat of material is defined as the quantity of heat required to raise temperature of unit mass of the material through 1 degree.

Unit: In C.G.S calories per gram per ?. In S.I. it is Joules per Kg per ?.

Specific heat at constant pressure (??):

It is defined as the amount of heat required to raise the temperature of unit mass of a gas through 1 ?, when its pressure is kept constant.

Specific heat at constant volume (??):

It is defined as the amount of heat required to raise the temperature of unit mass of a gas through 1 ??, when its volume is kept constant.

Relation between ?? and ??:

$$?? - ?? = ?$$

Where R is the universal gas constant.

?? ?? ??????? ???? ?? (?? > ??):

The heat is supplied to a gas and is allowed to expand at constant pressure. Then (i). It raises the temperature of the gas (i.e. increase in its internal energy)

(ii). It does work in expanding the gas against the external pressure

$dQ = dU + dW = dU + PdV$

When gas is heated at constant volume, no work is done ($dW = PdV = 0$) and hence whole of the heat supplied is used to raise its temperature. Thus more heat is required for increasing the temperature of the gas through 1 ?? at constant pressure than at constant volume. Hence ?? > ??.

------------- X --------------

EXERCISES

Multiple Choice Questions

1. Heat of an object is the .... energy of all the molecular motions inside that object.

    A) Average

    B) Total

    C) Minimum

    D) Zero

2. Temperature is a measure of the .... energy ofthe molecules.

    A) Binding

    B) Potential

    C) Thermal

    D) Gravitational

3. .... is the transfer of heat across a medium or objects which are in physical contact.

    A) Conduction

    B) Radiation

    C) Convection

    D) Absorption

4. Transfer of heat from a fluid to a solid surface or within a fluid is called ....

    A) Conduction

    B) Radiation

    C) Convection

    D) Absorption

5. Matter that is at finite temperature emits energy in space in the form of electromagnetic waves. The process is known as ....

A) Conduction

B) Radiation

C) Convection

D) Absorption

6. Heat radiation travels at the same speed as sound. (True/ **False**).

7. The Kelvin scale is an absolute scale. (**True**/ False)

8. Heat radiations cannot travel through a vacuum. (True / **False**)

9. Celsius temperature is defined to be exactly 273.15 less than the Kelvin temperature. (**True** / False)

10. Air conditioner is an example of radiation. (True / **False**)

Short Answer Questions

1. What is heat? Give SI unit of heat.

2. What is temperature? Give SI unit of temperature.

3. What are heat radiations? Whether these travel in straight line or not?

4. What is principle of measurement of temperature?

5. Define absolute zero of temperature?

6. What is triple point?

7. Give two examples of convection.

8. Define the process of conduction in metals.

9. Give relationship between Celsius and Fahrenheit scales of temperature.

10. Temperature of a patient is 40oC. What will be the corresponding temperature on Fahrenheit scale?

Long Answer Questions

1) Explain heat and temperature on basis of kinetic theory.

2) Describe principle of temperature measurements and name two such devices.

3) Describe with example different modes of transfer of heat.

4) Explain different scales of temperature and establish relationship between them.

5) Explain, what do you understand by absolute zero and triple point?

6) Give any five properties of heat radiations.